Financial Literacy and Inclusion in India

Financial Literacy and Inclusion in India

Edited by

Abdul Azeez N.P.
Assistant Professor, Department of Economics,
Aligarh Muslim University (AMU), Aligarh

and

S.M. Jawed Akhtar
Professor, Department of Economics,
Aligarh Muslim University (AMU), Aligarh

New Century Publications
New Delhi, India

NEW CENTURY PUBLICATIONS
4800 / 24, Bharat Ram Road,
Ansari Road, Daryaganj,
New Delhi - 110 002 (India)

Tel.: 011-2324 7798, 4358 7398, 4101 7798
E-mail: info@newcenturypublications.com
www.newcenturypublications.com

Editorial office:
LG – 7, Aakarshan Bhawan,
4754-57/23, Ansari Road, Daryaganj,
New Delhi – 110 002

Tel.: 011-4356 0919

First Published: **2019**

ISBN: **978-81-7708-484-9**

Published by New Century Publications and printed at Milan Enterprises, New Delhi.

Designs: Patch Creative Unit, New Delhi.

PRINTED IN INDIA

About the Book

Financial literacy deals with knowledge and skills which allow an individual to make informed and effective decisions with regard to his financial resources. An understanding of basic financial concepts allows people to navigate in the financial system successfully. People with financial literacy training make better financial decisions than those without it.

Financial literacy involves proficiency in financial principles, financial planning, debt management, saving techniques and the time value of money. Lack of financial literacy can lead to poor financial decisions including money loss, indebtedness and other negative consequences on the financial well-being of an individual.

The concept of financial inclusion has a special significance in India because a large segment of the society, particularly low-income earners, has little access to financial services, both formal and semi-formal. Resultantly, many of them have to depend either on their own or high cost informal sources of finance such as moneylenders. The essence of financial inclusion is to ensure that a range of appropriate financial services are available to all individuals to enable them to understand and access those services.

The present volume contains 8 research papers on financial literacy and financial inclusion authored by experts in the field. These scholarly contributions provide deep insights into the various aspects and problems associated with the twin policy goals of financial literacy and financial inclusion.

About the Editors

Dr. Abdul Azeez N.P. is currently Assistant Professor, Department of Economics at Aligarh Muslim University (AMU), Aligarh. Prior to joining AMU, he taught at the Department of Economics, Central University of Kashmir, Srinagar, Jammu and Kashmir. He also served as Assistant Professor (Economics) in the Department of Law at AMU, Malappuram Centre, Kerala.

A gold medallist of AMU in M.A. Economics (2010) examination, he obtained Ph.D. degree also from the same University. He also qualified the Junior Research Fellowship (JRF) examination conducted by University Grants Commission (UGC) in 2011. He has published 5 books and numerous research papers in reputed journals. He has participated and presented papers at various national and international conferences. Recently, he has been awarded a major research project on 'Digital and Financial Literacy for Rural India', funded by IMPRESS-ICSSR.

Dr. S.M. Jawed Akhtar is currently Professor, Department of Economics, Aligarh Muslim University (AMU), Aligarh. Presently, he is working as Finance Officer of AMU, Aligarh. He has been actively engaged in teaching and research for more than two decades. He was awarded gold medals for securing first position in B.A. (Hons.) and M.A. (Economics) examinations of the same University.

He has recently completed a major research project on Mahatma Gandhi National Rural Employment Guarantee Scheme (MGNREGS) funded by the UGC. He is also working as Co-Project Director on 'Digital and Financial Literacy for Rural India'. He has authored 12 books and published more than 60 research papers in academically acclaimed journals.

Contents

Contributors

Ashraf Pulikkamath Department of Economics, University of Madras, Chennai.

Muhammed Safwan A. Department of Economics, University of Madras, Chennai.

Subhashini Muthukrishnan Professor of Economics, Jain (Deemed to be University), Bengaluru.

Abdul Azeez N.P. Assistant Professor, Department of Economics, Faculty of Social Sciences, Aligarh Muslim University, Aligarh.

Nasira Banu M. Department of Economics, Faculty of Social Sciences, Aligarh Muslim University, Aligarh.

C. Krishnan Associate Professor of Economics, Government College Kodanchery, Kozhikode.

Muhammed Palath Visiting Faculty, Chair for Islamic Studies and Research, University of Calicut, Malappuram.

Sini VT Assistant Professor, Department of Commerce, MES Keveeyam College, Valanchery.

S.N. Tripathy Professor of Economics (Retd.), Gokhale Institute of Politics and Economics, Deccan Gymkhana, Pune.

M.H. Wani Professor, Rajiv Gandhi Chair, Sher-e-Kashmir University of Agricultural Sciences and Technology of Kashmir, Shalimar, Srinagar.

Arshad Bhat Assistant Professor, Rajiv Gandhi Chair, Sher-e-Kashmir University of Agricultural Sciences and Technology of Kashmir, Shalimar, Srinagar.

Preface

Financial literacy is the possession of a set of skills and knowledge which allows an individual to make informed and effective decisions with all of his financial resources. Understanding basic financial concepts allows people to know how to navigate in the financial system. People with appropriate financial literacy training make better financial decisions and manage money better than those without such training.

The book focuses on the ability to manage personal finance matters in an efficient manner, and it includes the knowledge of making appropriate decisions about personal finances such as investment, insurance, real estate, budgeting, retirement and tax planning. Financial literacy also involves the proficiency of financial principles and concepts such as financial planning, compound interest, managing debt, profitable savings techniques and the time value of money.

The main steps for achieving financial literacy include learning the skills to create a budget, the ability to track spending, learning the techniques to pay off debt and effectively planning for retirement. These steps can also include counselling from a financial expert. The contents of the book involve understanding how money works, creating and achieving financial goals and managing internal and external financial challenges.

There are many advantages of financial literacy. Financial literacy helps individuals to become self-sufficient so that they can achieve financial stability. Those who understand the subject should be able to answer several questions about purchases, such as whether an item is required, whether it is affordable, and whether it is an asset or a liability.

This skill can help a person in developing a financial road map to identify what he earns, what he spends and what he owes. The contents of the book also affect small business owners, who greatly contribute to economic growth and stability.

The lack of financial literacy can lead to owing large amounts of debt and making poor financial decisions. Similarly, financial illiteracy may lead to making poor financial choices that can have negative consequences on the financial well-being of an individual.

Financial illiteracy affects all ages at all socio-economic levels. Financial illiteracy causes many people to become victims of predatory lending, sub-prime mortgages, and fraud and high interest rates, potentially resulting in bad credit, bankruptcy or foreclosure.

The concept of financial inclusion has a special significance for a fast emerging economy such as India. In most developing countries, a large segment of the society, particularly low income people, has very little access to financial services, both formal and semi-formal. As a consequence, many of them have to necessarily depend either on their own or high cost informal sources of finance such as moneylenders. This is particularly true for the sporadic financing requirements of low income households for non-productive consumption purposes and other emergency requirements such as medical expenditure. Benefits of growth, therefore, tend to concentrate in the hands of those already served by the formal financial system.

According to the Committee on Financial Inclusion (Chairman: C. Rangarajan), 2008, "Financial inclusion may be defined as the process of ensuring access to financial services and timely and adequate credit where needed by vulnerable groups such as weaker sections and low income groups at an affordable cost".

The essence of financial inclusion is in trying to ensure that a range of appropriate financial services is available to every individual and enabling them to understand and access those services. Apart from the regular form of financial intermediation, it may include a basic no-frills banking account for making and receiving payments, a savings product suited to the pattern of cash flows of a poor household, money transfer facilities, small loans and overdrafts for productive, personal and other purposes, insurance (life and non-life) etc. While financial inclusion, in a narrow sense, may be achieved to some extent by offering any one of these services, the objective of *comprehensive financial inclusion* would be to provide a holistic set of services encompassing all of the above.

Indian economy in general and banking services in particular have made rapid strides in the recent past. However, a sizeable section of the population, particularly the vulnerable groups, such as weaker sections and low income groups, continue to remain excluded from even the most basic opportunities and services provided by the financial sector. Access to a well-functioning financial system, by creating equal opportunities, enables economically and socially excluded people to integrate better into the economy, so as to actively contribute to economic development and protect themselves against economic shocks.

Financial inclusion is a new paradigm of economic growth which plays a major role in driving away poverty. Lack of access to financial services in most of rural areas due to high informative barriers and low awareness, creates the need and scope of financial inclusion. Fruits of development have hardly reached nearly half of the Indian population because of lack of access to loans and insurance services. Financial inclusion is integral to the inclusive growth process and sustainable development of the country. It should, therefore, ideally be a policy of involving a much wider section of population.

Access to formal banking system is affected by several implementation and policy barriers such as culture, financial literacy, gender, income and assets, proof of identity, remoteness of residence etc. Over a period of time, several measures have been taken by the banks in India to improve access to affordable financial services through financial education, awareness generation, business communication networking and leveraging technology. The lack of awareness, low incomes and assets, social exclusion, illiteracy are the barriers from demand side. The distance from bank branch, branch timings, cumbersome banking procedure and requirements of documents for opening bank accounts, unsuitable banking products or schemes, language, high transaction costs and attitudes of bank officials are the barriers from the supply side. Hence, there is a need for financial inclusion to build uniform economic development through greater accessibility and transparency in fund-flow regime for ushering in greater economic and social equity.

There are several challenges that require concerted efforts from banks, the RBI and the Government to ensure convenient and cost-effective delivery of financial services to the public at large. In particular, the challenge is to introduce innovations in risk assessment, reduce transaction costs, devise new credit delivery channels, and use information technology to make financial inclusion a viable model. Looking at the immense potential lying ahead, rapid progress of financial inclusion efforts in India is the need of the hour.

The present volume contains 8 research papers on financial literacy and financial inclusion authored by experts in the field. These scholarly contributions provide deep insights into the various aspects and problems associated with the twin policy goals of financial literacy and financial inclusion.

We place on record our deep appreciation and gratefulness to the scholars who have contributed to this volume. We are confident that this attempt would surely add to the existing body of literature on the subject.

We sincerely thank the anonymous editors and production team of New Century Publications, New Delhi for standardizing and formatting the text in a professional and presentable manner.

Abdul Azeez N.P.
S.M. Jawed Akhtar

1

Financial Inclusion of Rural Daily Wage Earners

Ashraf Pulikkamath and Muhammed Safwan A.

Introduction

Financial inclusion is a vital tool in achieving inclusive growth and sustainable development. In most of the developing countries including India, a large segment of society, particularly low-income people, have very little access to financial services of both formal and semi-formal nature. Benefits of growth therefore tend to concentrate in the hands of those already well served by the formal financial system.

In spite of the rapid spread of banking and numerous financial inclusion schemes over the years, significant segment of our population, who are predominantly from the rural areas, is excluded from the formal financial system.

Banking institutions are primarily responsible for financial inclusion or financial exclusion. Though the banking industry in the country has shown tremendous growth during the last few decades, there are growing concerns that these banks have not been able to reach and bring vast segment of the population, especially the underprivileged sections of the society, into the fold of basic banking services, in spite of making significant improvements in all the areas relating to financial viability, profitability and competitiveness.

The role of a bank in case of inclusive finance has always been debated between what they can do and what they have done already in case of financial inclusion—which is primarily aimed at creating a platform for inculcating the habit to save money.

Usually, people in rural areas continue to live under the constant shadow of financial pressure mainly because of the absence of savings which makes them vulnerable to meet contingencies of life. In addition to inculcating a saving habit, financial inclusion would induce a move away from traditional modes of savings in land, buildings, bullion, etc., which will ultimately lead to capital formation in the country.

As another dimension of financial inclusion, providing formal credit avenues shall allow the entrepreneurial spirit of the masses to increase output and enhance prosperity in the countryside. Also, channelizing welfare programs of government such as subsidies through banks can be perceived as an effective tool to eradicate leakages and corruption. But where have we reached now? What have we achieved so far in this regard? These questions remain open to be answered. Hence, this paper becomes relevant in this era of 'Digital India' and 'Cashless Economy'.

Objectives of the Study

- To understand the status of financial inclusion among rural people.
- To understand various hazards that blocks access of daily wage earners to financial inclusion.
- To understand the awareness and reach of the national inclusion policy viz. 'Pradhan Mantri Jan DhanYojna'.

Sources of Data and Methodology

The research methodology adopted for carrying the study was mainly designed as a descriptive work based on primary and secondary data. Respondents in this study included daily wage earners from 4 rural villages in Malappuram district of Kerala, namely, Anakkayam, Kizhattur, Melattur and Koottilangadi and the purposive sampling method was employed to collect the data. Malappuram is one of the backward districts in Kerala and it has a predominant Muslim population who are again one of the most backward communities in the country (Sachar Committee Report, 2005).

Primary data of 120 respondents was collected from these 4 villages and they were analyzed and presented using the basic statistical methods.

Financial inclusion means bringing the disadvantaged and low-income segments of the society in the coverage of financial services, in contrast to financial exclusion where those services are not available or affordable. Though Ernakulum district of Kerala was declared as the first fully financial inclusive district of India (2012), the case is not the same in rural areas. Most of the recent studies in this regard show that still there are a number of people who have never been a part of the financial inclusion movement and it is noteworthy that they are mostly dealing with the unorganized sector. Meanwhile, there is another segment of people who may never join the formal financial system like banking due to certain cultural and religious matters, which is also more prevalent in rural areas.

Review of Literature

Maniklal and Supravat (2010) observed that the socio-economic traits are the determinants of financial exclusion and inclusion. They suggest implementation of SHG-Bank Linkage or co-operative linkage more intensively in rural areas in order to accelerate financial inclusion. Joseph (2010) establishes that financial institutions have a very critical role in fostering financial inclusion. Lack of financial literacy is a major hindrance in spreading financial inclusion. This has resulted in more than 50 percent of savings of the household sector and of the financially illiterate getting drained in non-financial investments. Maini (2010) observed that the Responsible Finance Initiative, cross-linked to the financing could help improve management, governance, operational practices and disclosure.

Hema (2013) found that there is greater need to educate and create some new instruments for daily wage earners and also make them a part of financial inclusion by examining the impact of financial inclusion on daily wage earners. Hemaand

Kumar (2012) also found that the financial system in India has grown rapidly in the last three decades. The functional and geographical coverage of the system is truly impressive. There is an imperative need to modify the credit and financial services delivery system to achieve greater inclusion. While banks and other financial institutions can also take some efforts on their own to improve the absorptive capacity of the clients, it is equally important for the government at various levels to initiate actions to enhance the earning capacity of the poorer sections of the society with special reference to daily wage earners and there is greater need to create awareness and educate them on these lines.

Sharmah and Horen (2014) observed that financial inclusion has made inroads among the daily wage earners of tea industry. The pace or speed of inclusion may not be a robust one but a humble beginning has been made which is bold, powerful and purposeful. The study also felt the need to educate daily wage earners and a great deal of publicity about different existing instruments of financial inclusion should be undertaken by the appropriate agencies. Most of the tea gardens are located in remote places and the distance to the nearest bank is one of the major hurdles for these workers to reap the benefits of financial inclusion. Therefore, banks should make sincere efforts to open their outlets near the tea gardens. Precisely, it is concluded that there is an enhanced need to educate daily wage earners about new instruments which form a part of financial inclusion.

Ananth and Sabri (2013) insist that, though both public and private sector banks are subject to the same norms, our reasons for emphasizing the role of public sector banks are three. Public sector banks have a much larger presence in unbanked areas, they face more political pressure than private banks and they play a much larger role in government sponsored poverty alleviation schemes. The challenges to expand financial inclusion in India are structural and they have often negated the various incremental measures that have been taken towards this.

Thus, they conclude that the ultimate success of financial inclusion would depend on: (a) measures that expand the scope of the formal banking sector; (b) overcoming pervading information asymmetries; (c) expanding financial literacy through state programs (neither public nor private banks will be able to bear the costs); (d) mandating appropriate agencies to lead efforts that expand financial inclusion; and (e) creating a relevant set of financial products that meet the needs of the financially excluded.

The Discussion

To start with, it is suitable to look at national financial inclusion policy named Pradhan Mantri Jan Dhan Yojna (PMJDY). It is a national mission for financial inclusion in order to ensure access of financially excluded people to financial services, namely, savings and deposit accounts, remittance, credit, insurance, and pension in an affordable manner. It is a great initiative by the government to provide better banking services in villages, so as to improve participation of a large chunk of rural population in different plans launched by government from time to time.

Bank accounts can be opened in any bank branch or business correspondent (Bank Mitra) outlet under this scheme and those accounts can be opened and operated with zero balance. However, if the account holder wishes to get cheque book, he/she will have to fulfil the minimum balance criteria. Further, the scheme has provisions for many other benefits including interest on deposit, accidental insurance cover of ₹ 1 lakh, life insurance cover of ₹ 30,000, and overdraft facility up to ₹ 5,000.

Table 1.1 explains the current status of the PMJDY scheme in Kerala. It is evident that the number of urban or metro category accounts is almost ¼ times higher than that of rural accounts, which is not a good indicator for any financial inclusion scheme. This is a proof of the concerns marked in the literature that the advantaged and urban people enjoy the benefits of financial inclusion mostly and the rural segment of population who are predominantly working in the unorganized sector on daily basis earning are excluded in this regard. However, the rural-urban disparity is not so in national figures, where the number of rural accounts are much higher than the urban accounts.

Table 1.1: Number of Accounts Opened under PMJDY in Kerala (October 2017)

Rural accounts	Urban accounts	Total accounts	Deposit (₹ crore)	Rupay card issued
17,53,853	22,22,499	39,76,352	1,130.38	28,93,957

Source: Ministry of Finance, Government of India.

This is where the Kerala scenario is noteworthy, because it is a state which has been marked by many admirable achievements. But in case of financial inclusion, data shows that the state has not considered the inclusion of rural community seriously when still 53 percent (2011 Census) of its population belongs to the rural category.

Table 1.2 summarizes the socio-economic characteristics of the respondents of this study. Majority of the respondents were males in the 20-40 age group and who predominantly belonged to the Muslim community. This can be read in connection with the fact that the Malappuram District of Kerala is a Muslim-dominated district where 71 percent (Census 2011) of the total population belonged to the Muslim community. Almost 75 percent of the respondents were married and half of the respondents were having educational qualification below 10th standard and half of them were above 10th standard. It again points out to the fact that the community is less educated compared to the general context of Kerala. It also means an increase in their economic risk due to family affiliation and lesser educational qualifications. However, a majority of them (71 percent) earn a good daily wage, say ₹ 400-₹ 600 or above (only 3 percent), indicating higher wages in the state compared to other parts of the country. Strictly speaking, these high wages should reflect in the economic well-being of such people and their families.

Table 1.2: Socio-economic Features of Respondents

Features	Sub Features	Frequency	Percentage
Age	Below 20	9	7.5
	20-40	84	70.0
	40-60	23	19.2
	Above 60	4	3.3
	Total	120	100.0
Gender	Male	95	79.2
	Female	25	20.8
	Total	120	100.0
Religion	Hindu	41	34.2
	Muslim	75	62.5
	Christian	4	3.3
	Total	120	100.0
Marital status	Single	31	25.8
	Married	89	74.2
	Total	120	100.0
Education level	Below 5th Std	5	4.2
	5th to 10th	53	44.2
	above 10th	62	51.7
	Total	120	100.0
Daily earning	Below ₹ 200	1	0.8
	₹ 200-₹ 400	31	25.8
	₹ 400-₹ 600	85	70.8
	Above ₹ 600	3	2.5
	Total	120	100.0

Source: Primary Data.

Awareness about anything is gateway to access for a service or facility. Financial inclusion is no exception in this regard. According to Table 1.3, almost 83 percent of the respondents were aware about a basic savings account whereas only 23 percent of them had actually availed of the facility, indicating lesser reach of basic banking services for the rural segment of population. None of the respondents had availed an entrepreneurial credit, over draft and credit card facilities though some of them were aware of such facilities. It is established that the rural community has never been taught to move out of the daily wage earning system or move into a better entrepreneurial life.

Table 1.3: Awareness and Access to Basic Financial Inclusion Components

Financial Inclusion Components	Aware	Percentage	Availed	Percentage
Savings bank account	100	83.3	27	22.5
Entrepreneurial credit	55	45.8	0	0.0
Small overdraft	30	25.0	0	0.0
Insurance	110	91.7	48	40.0
Credit card	30	25.0	0	0.0
Bank loan	114	95.0	30	25.0
ATM card	117	97.5	27	22.5
Mobile banking/net banking	79	65.8	15	12.5
Bank account linked subsidy/schemes	102	85.0	18	15.0

Source: Primary Data.

ATM, bank loan and insurance were the most well know components and that in spite, most of them had not availed the same. It is obvious that these facilities would not come without an operational bank account. Say for example, only 40 percent of the respondents availed insurance although 92 percent of the respondents were aware of it. This signifies that they are aware of the risk factor of life, but yet could not afford insurance due to some reasons. Mobile or net banking was also availed of by only 13 percent of the respondents, in spite of the fact that 80 percent of them were aware about it. Bank account linked financial assistance schemes also witnessed a lower outreach at 15 percent due to lack of bank accounts.

Banking sector in an area has the primary responsibility in ensuring the success of financial inclusion activities. Thus, banking institutions are supposed to act accordingly irrespective of their category of entity. However, the actual picture of performance with regards to bank accounts depicts a key role played by the public sector banks. As per Table 1.4, around 75 percent of the account holders (out of 23 percent of total respondents) were having a bank account and 50 percent of such accounts were in public sector banks. Another 25 percent of accounts belonged to regional rural banks and cooperative banks, whereas private sector banks contributed a mere 25 percent on such kind of accounts. This is evident of the fact that banks—except public sector banks—are not approachable for the rural community yet, though they are equally responsible for financial inclusion agenda. A considerable size of the rural community (26 percent) is still out of the banking network and they hold their savings in non-banking institutions.

Table 1.4: Bank, Non-bank and Type of Bank

Type of bank	Bank type	Frequency	Percentage
Bank	**Bank**	20	74.07
	-Public sector	10	50.00
	-Private sector	5	25.00
	-Regional rural	3	15.00
	-Co-operative	2	10.00
Non-bank	**Non-bank**	7	25.93

Source: Primary Data.

Access to credit is crucial while talking about financial inclusion practices, because it saves people from the vulnerabilities of economic uncertainties. However, the real scenario of the rural community is not appreciable at all. As explained by Table 1.5, almost 70 percent of the respondents had a non-bank credit service against 25 percent who had bank credits. This is a huge difference while seriously talking about rural financial inclusion. These rural communities are mostly borrowing from money lenders (61 percent) who economically exploit them throughout their life. In addition, 82 percent of them are dependent on their friends to meet emergency crisis. These figures show the depth of financial vulnerability of rural people during uncertainties in their life. Additionally, these people constantly live under the shadow of uncertainties backed by unorganized working and earning pattern. Somehow, 20 percent of them are having support from SHGs in this regard.

Table 1.5: Sources of Credit

Source of accessing credit	Frequency	Percent	Non-bank source of accessing credit	Frequency	Percent
Bank	30	25.00	—	—	—
Non-bank	82	68.33	SHG	17	20.73
			Friends	68	82.93
			Money Lenders	50	60.98

Source: Primary Data.

Why do people choose to go beyond formal credit avenues? Table 1.6 refers to possible reasons for people to go for non-banking credit avenues. Approximately, 50 percent of the respondents believe that informal channels have an easy accessibility. No security requirements and least time of processing attract people (35-39 percent) to the non-banking ventures for borrowing, the table explains. Lastly, 9 percent of the respondents agreed that they are financially illiterate to approach such formal channels of credit. It is surprising to see such a sizeable population in a state like Kerala where literacy rate is 100 percent.

Table 1.6: Reasons for Non-bank Source of Credit

Reason to choose non-bank credit	Frequency	Percent
No security requirement	46	38.33
Easy availability	59	49.17
Less time requirement	42	35.00
Financial illiteracy	10	8.33

Source: Primary Data..

Having appreciation about something is an indication that a particular person or community is likely to accept and make use of the things they appreciate. While coming to the financial inclusion aspect and capability of securing life, more than half of the rural community is doubtful (Table 1.7). It can be perceived due to lack of proper awareness about the benefits of financial inclusion and lack of financial literacy. This scenario marks a picture of financial excluded rural India, even in a literate state like Kerala. The detachment with banking might also be related to the Muslim orthodoxy in this region (Table 1.8).

Table 1.7: Financial Inclusion Assistance in Securing Future Help

Is financial inclusion helpful?	Frequency	Percent
Yes	57	47
No	63	53

Source: Primary Data.

Finally, the reach of PMJDY as explained in the beginning should not be ignored. Among the rural respondents, 66 percent of them were aware of the scheme while only 25 percent of them had actually availed the same. In other words, 75 percent of the rural community still stands out of the umbrella of PMJDY, indicating that an increase in number of PMJDY accounts are not compatible with the actual target groups of the scheme. Those increases in the PMJDY accounts are thus artificial or technical, such as additional accounts for people who had accounts already or just the inclusion of urban community alone motivated by the proximity of banking institutions.

Table 1.8: Awareness and Reach of PMJDY

Awareness/Access	Frequency	Percent
Aware	79	66
Unaware	41	34
Availed	19	24.05
Not Availed	60	75.95

Source: Primary Data.

Conclusion

Since the development of bottom segment of the society is a key for overall economic development, the study was an attempt to find out the status of financial inclusion scheme among daily wage earners. The bottom segment of the society is mainly comprised of daily wage earners or those who have no regular and systematic way of earning. So, banking facilities and timely availability of credit at an affordable cost have to play a bigger role in contributing to the well-being of the weaker sections of the society.

This study makes it clear that most of the rural daily wage earners are aware but they are still hesitating to avail such financial inclusion services. Lack of knowledge about various financial inclusion services complimented by the complex banking process is major difficulties found in accessing financial inclusion services. Much in the same way like other financial inclusion schemes, majority of the respondents were aware about PMJDY and its benefits, but a very few actually subscribed to the same. Thus, it is suggested that the authorities take necessary steps to convert public awareness about various financial inclusion services into actual practice. In addition, complications in banking services should be simplified and it will be great if the concerned authorities can arrange people to assist the rural community regarding various financial schemes.

References

Ananth, Sabri (2013), "Challenges to Financial Inclusion in India: The Case of Andhra Pradesh", *Economic and Political Weekly*, 4(7).

Hema, P. (2013), "A Study on Impact of Financial Inclusion With Reference To Daily Wage Earners", *Journal of Business Management and Social Science Research*, 2(6), 2319-5614.

Joseph, L. (2010), "Role of Financial Institutions in Financial Inclusion", *FICCI-Banking and Finance Journal*, 3(4).

Kumar, Hema (2012), "Financial Inclusion: Offering Banking Services for the Poor", *International Journal of Banking and Finance*, 1(2).

Maini, T. (2010), "Financial Inclusion: The Way Forward", *FICCI-Banking and Finance Journal*, 3(4).

Manaiklal, Supravat (2010), "Impact of SHGs on Financial Inclusion: A Case Study in the District of Bankura", *Journal of Applied Finance and Banking*, 2(2), 1792-6580.

Nair, S. (2010), "Financial Inclusion: Innovative Approaches", *FICCI-Banking and Finance Journal*, 3(4).

Prasanta, Horen (2014), "Financial Inclusion on Daily Wage Earners in Tea Garden of Assam: Challenges and Remedial Measures", *International Journal of Research and Development in Technology and Management Science*, 21(5).

2

Banking Habits and Access to Formal Credit

Subhashini Muthukrishnan

Access to a variety of financial products and services is related to financial inclusion which in itself is an issue in developing countries like India as banks are the major providers of various financial services and products. Individuals and households require credit for a variety of reasons and when they are unable to get credit from formal sources due to financial exclusion, they fall prey to local moneylenders who offer credit at very high rates of interest. It is assumed that individuals who have a bank account have access to debit cards, credit cards and insurance which may not be true for all account holders.

Factors like low income, level of education, gender, caste, lack of financial literacy, not having the required documents to open a bank account or complex processes involved in opening an account and geographical distance, makes access to formal credit difficult. The banking habits of people are affected by several factors ranging from gender, occupation, availability of easy short-term credit from relatives and friends and banks' support in providing loans. In 2017, public sector banks provided 39.5 percent of the priority sector lending, while private banks provided 42.5 percent and foreign banks 36.4 percent. This was quite unchanged in 2018 as the numbers stood at 39.9 percent for public sector banks, 40.8 percent for private banks and 38.3 percent for foreign banks. This paper thus examines the various dimensions of banking habits among people.

Review of the Literature

Economists hold different views on the role of finance and

its relationship with long-run economic growth. Alexander Hamilton (1781) stated that banks were invented for advancing trade which promotes growth. The Schumpeterian view of finance and development highlights the impact of banks on productivity growth (Schumpeter, 1934). Patrick (1966) states that financial sector assists in transferring resources from the traditional, low growth sectors to the modern, high growth sectors and stimulate an entrepreneurial response in these modern sectors. Hicks (1969) posited that financial structures are relevant for trend growth and for shaping the business cycle around the trend. Goldsmith (1969) showed the presence of a positive correlation between the size of the financial system and long-run economic growth.

Shaw (1973) stated the role of financial intermediaries in transmitting loanable funds between spending units thus deepening in economic growth. Romer (1986) and Lucas (1988) highlighted the role of financial development for long-run economic growth in developing countries. Thus, development of the financial system contributes to economic growth (Rajan and Zingales, 2003).

Empirical literature indicates to the many facets of financial inclusion and banking habits. Chase, Gjertson and Collins (2011) identify reasons of household's inability to save and its consequences like turning to friends, family and potentially even to public subsidy programs for short-term credit. At times, they even sell possessions, or seek a formal or informal loan. Chattopadhyay's (2011) survey in West Bengal revealed that absence of collateral security prevents households from borrowing from banks and meet their requirements from moneylenders who charge exorbitantly high rates of interest. Sparreboom and Duflos' (2012) study in China revealed that the poorest still do not have access to basic banking services and depend on non-bank providers such as guarantee companies and pawnshops for credit.

Mowl's (2012) study found that majority of India's high personal savings are invested in physical assets, and thus most of the borrowing is relegated to the informal credit market. Time loss due to travel, waiting period and documentation requirements are a substantial burden to borrowing from the formal sources. Ananth (2013) emphasized that the success of financial inclusion depends on expansion of public sector banks in rural space and their role in providing suitable financial products to rural population. A study by Triki and Faye (2013) on financial inclusion in Africa found that many adults in Africa use informal methods to save such as Rotating Savings and Credit Associations (ROSCAs), chit funds, burial societies and borrow from friends, family, and informal private lenders.

Brown, Castañeda, Cloke and Taylor (2013) found that men are more likely to access financial services from the formal financial sector than women. Exclusion also happens because of easy access to family and friends for convenient low cost loans and convenience of alternative arrangements. Ananth and Sabri (2013) found that the quantity of loans created by the banking system is generally a function of both the willingness and ability of banks to lend.

We now discuss access to formal financial institutions and then present some general observations in the end.

Data Sources

This paper is based on a field survey conducted using a schedule in the two districts of Karnataka namely Bangalore urban and Bangalore rural in 2014. Data was collected from 1,049 respondents from railway stations, bus stops, village markets, residential areas and from different areas of these two districts. Sources of credit were classified into formal and informal lenders, reasons for opening a bank account and borrowing, agents assisting in opening an account, usage of credit and debit cards, seeking financial advice are some of the important variables used in the study. The data collected has been analyzed using descriptive statistics and using the probit model.

Descriptive Statistics

This set of findings relate to descriptive statistics.

Agents Assisting in Financial Inclusion: Different economic agents help in opening bank accounts. In the survey, we found that of the 695 respondents who had bank accounts, 67.2 percent were assisted by friends and family to open bank accounts. Village panchayat officials could help only 0.3 percent and bank officials (17.1 percent) and 2.7 percent did not get any help to open a bank account. This indicates that banks can play a more motivating role in helping the unbanked to open bank accounts by using social network channels like family and friends. Banks too must act in a more proactive manner to help individuals open bank accounts.

Reasons for Opening Account: Everyone who ever can save, saves irrespective of having a formal financial tool. People open a bank account for a variety of purposes. Listing the reasons for opening accounts in rural and urban areas, we found that of the 66.3 percent of respondents who had bank accounts, 67.8 percent of urban respondents opened a bank account for saving purpose while the number was only 45.9 percent in rural areas. Data reveals that requesting for loan is higher in urban areas standing at 19.2 percent while in rural areas it was 3.8 percent.

Moreover, 18.2 percent had opened account for receiving payments of which 24.9 percent were from urban areas while 7.3 percent were from rural areas. In the urban areas, 26.3 percent of the respondents opened an account for making remittances and a lower figure of 23.7 percent for receiving remittances. This was reverse for the rural respondents—for receiving remittances being higher at 10.6 percent while making remittances being lower at 6.0 percent. In urban areas, 22.5 percent account holders used banking services to make payments for purchases while this figure stood at only 1.3 percent for the rural areas. This depicts that banks can increase their presence in rural areas and increase the use of debit cards and other instruments for making payments.

Reasons For Not Having A Bank Account: Financial exclusion happens due to a variety of factors. This survey attempted to capture a couple of factors that exclude people from formal banking services. From the total of 33.7 percent who were financially excluded, the most important reason for their exclusion was inadequate money to participate in the formal banking system (15.1 percent), followed by 9.1 percent who use their spouse's account, and 3.1 percent who stated that they do not have banking habit and 2.5 percent opined as having no specific reason.

The above mentioned are the pre-dominant reasons for not having a bank account. Other than these reasons, there were some institutional restrictions as well. For example, in order to open a bank account people require identification documents (6 percent). 0.6 percent respondents stated that they tried opening bank accounts but were refused, 0.5 percent said they saw no point in opening an account as they were receiving benefits in cash. Interestingly, none said that they could not open an account due to the minimum amount to be kept in banks or because they had a bad credit history. All these reasons taken together, it was observed that at least 4 percent of people did not open bank account for these reasons (Table 2.1).

Table 2.1: Reasons for Not Having a Bank Account

Access/Exclusion	
Not excluded	695 (66.3)
Lack of money	158 (15.1)
Lack of habit	32 (3.1)
Using spouse's account	95 (9.1)
Do not know	26 (2.5)
All other factors	43 (4)
Total	1,049 (100)

Note: Figures in the parentheses indicate percentages.
Source: Collated from field work.

Factors Affecting Borrowing

One of the important dimensions that affect financial

inclusion is the ability to borrow from formal sources of credit. 40.9 percent of the total respondents had taken a loan while 59.1 percent had not borrowed. From this situation we found that in urban areas, 37.4 percent had borrowed while in rural areas 46.6 percent had borrowed. Table 2.2 presents a compilation of the various socio-economic factors that determine borrowing.

Table 2.2: Socio-economic Factors Affecting Borrowing

		Borrowed during the last one year		Total
		Yes	No	
Gender	Male	225 (43.8)	289 (56.2)	514 (100.0)
	Female	204 (38.1)	331 (61.9)	535 (100.0)
Caste	SC	50 (33.6)	99 (66.4)	149 (100.0)
	ST	20 (42.6)	27 (57.4)	47 (100.0)
	OBCs	74 (55.6)	59 (44.4)	133 (100.0)
	General	273 (40.1)	408 (59.9)	681 (100.0)
	Others	12 (30.8)	27 (69.2)	39 (100.0)
Religion	Hindu	364 (40.4)	536 (59.6)	900 (100.0)
	Muslim	34 (46.6)	39 (53.4)	73 (100.0)
	Christian	27 (38.6)	43 (61.4)	70 (100.0)
	Others	4 (66.7)	2 (33.3)	6 (100.0)
Region	Urban	243 (37.3)	408 (62.7)	651 (100.0)
	Rural	186 (46.7)	212 (53.3)	398 (100.0)

Note: Figures in the parentheses indicate percentages.
Source: collated from field work.

From the table, we see that males borrowed more (43.8 percent) while only 38.1 percent females borrowed. Among the caste groups, the group that borrowed the highest during the year in consideration were the OBCs households at 55.6 percent followed by STs at 42.6 percent, general category at 40.1 percent and SCs at 33.6 percent. Among the religious groups, the group that borrowed the highest during the last year were the Muslim households at 46.6 percent followed by Hindu households at 40.4 percent, and Christian households at 38.6 percent. Respondents belonging to other religions like Budhism and Jainism were few in the sample.

Among those who borrowed, 69.9 percent experienced no major difficulties after borrowing whereas 27.6 percent were unable to keep track of date and amount to be repaid and were very much worried about the fact that they are getting into a debt trap. 47.1 percent respondents said that in case of emergency they will borrow from family or friends. Again, it is clear that formal financial sector is unable to meet peoples' demand for money in emergency situations which forces them to borrow from the informal sector. Formal financial sector has to devise financial products then can serve this need of the society.

Distribution of Borrowing by Source

It is common place that most borrowing occurs through informal sources, such as family, friends, money lenders and others besides banks. Of the total respondents, 40.9 percent had taken a loan while 59.1 percent stated that they had not taken a loan during the last one year. Among those 42.2 percent who had borrowed, only 12.2 percent borrowed from the banks and in aggregate 25.1 percent people took loans from the informal sector including from friends (3.3 percent), relatives (6.9 percent), money lenders (5.3 percent), and other sources (9.6 percent). Moreover, 3.6 percent people availed loan from more than one source. Therefore, we can conclude that people depend more on the informal sector than the formal sector for accessing credit.

Reasons for Borrowing from Informal Sources

Borrowers look for lenders who are easy to access in terms of documents, time and effort. From the sample, we found that out of a total of 1,049 respondents 18.7 percent stated that money lenders provide small sums that they require without much hassle.

Often, lenders in this sector do not require a guarantee or other security (17.4 percent). 0.5 percent of the respondents felt that informal borrowing is convenient for them. Repayment (6.8 percent) methods also make accessing loans from this informal sector easier for them than from the formal sector. Besides that, lenders in the informal sector are known persons (1.8 percent) and hence loans are provided easily and also locally (9.9 percent).

From this analysis, it can be implied that banks need to devise methods and products which will make them an attractive destination for seeking loans. Also, the behavioural aspect of banks in facilitating lending is necessary.

People borrow to meet a variety of needs. With such low incomes and rising cost of living, many borrow (27.5 percent) to tide over the monetary needs to meet day to day expenses. Also the socio-cultural background demands expenditure on a variety of personal expenditure (51.5 percent) for which banks may not be willing to lend. The increasing consumerism and the availability of newer household gadgets also make people (25.4 percent) borrow to buy these goods. Building a house is yet another important reason for people to borrow (20.3 percent). Rural and urban indebtedness is yet another important reason for people to borrow. They take fresh loans to repay off old loans (8.9 percent). All these indicate that the diverse socio-cultural and economic needs influence the formal sector to be pragmatic, innovative yet cautious in giving loans to people and prevent them from getting trapped in the informal sector.

Different households have different financial requirements which are often determined by a households' income level. By distributing the income level of the households into four categories, it was observed that out of 40.9 percent respondents who had borrowed for several reasons, 62.9 percent of them took personal loans with household income of ₹ 1,20,000-₹ 1,80,000 per annum. The richest section in the sample were households with income level of ₹ 3,60,000 and above demanding loans for building houses (38 percent) and to purchase vehicles (11.7 percent). The poorest income group with household income less than ₹ 1,20,000 borrowed mainly to purchase household items (34.3 percent) and to meet day to day living expenses (39 percent).

Data shows that 75.4 percent of the respondents were not refused any loan during the past three years and 5.4 percent of the respondents said they were refused a loan during the last one year. 72.4 percent of the respondents said they did not have any trouble with the loan they had taken and were able to repay them but 21.4 percent respondents found it difficult to pay back the loan on time and the amount to be paid. 15.8 percent did not answer the question. Moreover, 69.9 percent said that they are very much worried about the fact that they were getting into a debt.

47.1 percent respondents opined that in case of emergency, they will take money from family or friends. Again, it is clear that formal financial sector is unable to meet peoples' demand for money in emergency situations which forces them to borrow more from the informal sector. This is shown in Table 2.3 below.

Table 2.3: Financial Support during an Emergency

	No	Yes	Total
Ask family or friends	171 (16.3)	878 (83.7)	1,049 (100)
Draw upon savings	664 (63.3)	385 (36.7)	1,049 (100)
Sell something	1,018 (97)	31 (3)	1,049 (100)
Borrow from other sources	1,021 (97.3)	28 (2.7)	1,049 (100)
Use credit card	1,021 (97.3)	28 (2.7)	1,049 (100)
Don't know	1,022 (97.4)	27 (2.6)	1,049 (100)
Others	1,036 (98.8)	13 (1.20)	1,049 (100)

Note: Figures in the parentheses indicate percentages.

Source: Collated from field work.

Access to Insurance

Financial inclusion has another important dimension, namely access to insurance. Access to insurance reduces uncertainty and helps people to carry on normal activities and take suitable business risks without the fear of other kind of uncertainties like health issues, loss of property and accidents. In the survey, we found that 52.3 percent had some form of insurance. As far as gender aspect of insurance is concerned, we found that while 61 percent males had insurance of one form or the other, only 39 percent females had insurance. When it comes to life insurance, 57.4 percent males and 42.6 percent females had this form of insurance. 41.8 percent women had health insurance while 58.2 percent men had health insurance. In case of vehicle insurance, 77.8 percent males and 22.2 percent females had this form of insurance. Only 25.7 percent in rural areas had insurance while 74.3 percent in urban areas had insurance which again points out that access to financial products like insurance is limited in rural areas. All this indicates to the fact that not only is insurance as a financial product available and taken by many but also it is gendered and regionally biased against rural areas.

To the question why they did not opt for insurance indicated that out of 1,049 respondents, 26.2 percent said they did not feel the need for insurance, followed by 13.4 percent who said it was expensive, and 6.3 percent stated that there is no real reason for not having an insurance. 1.4 percent felt that they had nothing valuable to insure. This attitude towards insurance indicates that this is a major area where financial inclusion must step in and reduce the vagaries of life of people by providing insurance products and by also providing advice on the need of getting insured.

Other Financial Products and Services

Financial inclusion also means the availability and usage of other financial products besides banking and insurance. This includes use of technology in banking in order to increase access and reduce cost of transactions. There are many formal financial products available in the financial market such as credit cards, debit cards, mobile banking, and net banking facilities among others.

Debit Card Usage: Debit card is a technology dependent financial product which increases accessibility to finance. It reduces cost of visiting banks and is usable at any time. 580 respondents or 55.3 percent of the sample used debit cards. Among the users, 58.8 percent were males while 41.2 percent were females. Of the total 55.3 percent users, 74.1 percent users were in urban areas while only 25.9 percent used debit card in rural areas. 29 percent respondents with a degree level education, 14.1 percent with post-graduate level education, 17.6 percent with pre-university level and 33.4 percent with a SSLC level of education used these cards. When we examined the proximity of a bank and the use of debit card, we found that of the 55.3 percent users, 45 percent had a bank branch within a radius of 2-5 kilometres, 44.3 percent had it within 1 kilometre, and 9.5 percent had it within a 6-10 kilometre radius from their place of residence. Of the users, 78.6 percent had accounts with scheduled banks and 124 (21.4 percent) did not have accounts with the scheduled banks. 138 (23.8 percent) had accounts with the private banks. Only 4.1 percent or 24 respondents had account with cooperative banks as regards the use of debit cards.

Credit Card Usage: Data shows that only 11.7 percent people used a credit card. Of the total 123 respondents who used credit cards, 58.5 percent were males and 41.5 percent were females. Of these 11 percent respondents, 83.75 percent were Hindus, 12.2 percent were Christians and 3.3 percent were Muslims, whereas others constituted only 0.8 percent.

61 percent were employed in the private sector while 16.3 percent were in the government sector. 10.6 percent were casual laborers possibly using some form of credit card and 6 percent were agriculturists. Degree holders formed the largest group using the credit cards at 48.0 percent followed by post-graduates at 28.5 percent, SSLCs at 13.8 percent, and pre-university level at 9.8 percent.

Mobile Banking Usage: A total of 108 or 10.3 percent respondents used mobile banking. Among this, 68.5 percent were males while 31.5 were females. The use of mobile banking was largely urban based with 91.7 percent users from urban areas while only 8.3 percent from rural areas. The level of education was an important determinant of mobile banking usage. 49.1 percent respondents with degree level of education, 35.2 percent with post-graduate level, 9.3 percent with pre-university level and 5.6 percent with SSLC level of education used mobile banking.

Among the users, 75 percent were employed in the private sector, 13 percent in the government, 7.4 percent were casual labourers, 3.7 percent were currently unemployed and 0.9 percent were agriculturalists. Of the respondents, 63.9 percent had accounts with scheduled banks, 41.7 percent had accounts with private banks, and 7.4 percent had accounts with cooperative banks. Out of the total 10.3 percent users of mobile banking facilities, 97.2 percent of them had a savings account, 10.2 percent had a current account, 4.6 percent had a recurring account and 7.4 percent had a fixed deposit account. As far as distance from the bank is concerned, 41.7 percent of the 108 respondents used mobile banking with banks less than 1 kilometre, 41 percent with banks within 6 kilometres, and 13.9 percent having banks within 6-10 kilometres.

Net Banking Usage: 84 respondents or 8 percent from the sample used net banking services. Of this, 95.2 percent were in urban areas and only 4.8 percent in rural areas; 67.9 percent were males while 32.1 percent were females. 75.0 percent of the respondents worked in the private sector, 14.3 percent in government, 3.6 percent were unemployed, 6 percent were casual laborers and 1.2 percent was agriculturists. The last two category responses do not appear to be convincing though. Like in the case of users of mobile banking, net banking users too were the educated lot with 50 percent holding a degree, 36.9 percent post-graduates, 8.3 percent pre-university level, and 4.8 percent SSLC. This clearly shows that usage of technology driven inclusion can happen only with a rise in education level. 65.5 percent of the net users had an account with scheduled banks while 45.2 percent had accounts with private sector banks, and 7.1 percent with cooperative banks. 98.8 percent net banking users held a savings bank account. Of the users, 44 percent had banks within a 1 kilometre radius, 42.9 percent within 5 kilometre and 11.9 percent within a 6-10 kilometre radius.

Financial Advice: Seeking financial advice on financial matters is yet another dimension of financial inclusion. People may have money to save or may require a loan, however they do not often approach the formal sector due to lack of knowledge about various products available from the formal financial sector. In the sample, 628 respondents or 59.9 percent had sought financial advice. In this category, 56.4 percent took financial advice from their family members, 33 percent from friends, 1.4 percent from banks and 1.7 percent from financial advisers and others. When asked to express their level of interest in seeking local financial advice, on a scale of 1-5, 25.8 percent respondents stated that they were very interested in seeking financial advice and only 8.7 percent were not at all interested in seeking such an advice.

To understand the level of awareness about bank facilities, questions were asked about a respondent's knowledge about zero balance account. It was discovered that only 24.9 percent of the respondents came to know about this from bank officials and the rest from SHGs, NGOs, neighbors, posters, newspapers and others comprising the rest. 78.4 percent people did not have any information about the existence of a "no frills account". Only 10.3 percent came to know about it from bank officials and 3.5 percent from advertisements. Lack of information also excludes people from the use of financial products. There is, thus, an urgent need of creating awareness about banks and several facilities available to the people so that financial inclusion from the demand side can be enhanced.

Econometric Specification

The regression models considered in this study had a

dichotomous dependent variable. In other words, the dependent variable assumes a value of 1 if individual respondents have reported positively in regards to our research question; 0 value has been assigned otherwise. There were five regression equations altogether. The first model provided the determinant of financial inclusion. A household was considered as financially included if an individual possessed a bank account.

The second model tried to address the problem of credit inclusion (i.e. determinants of availing credit). In this context, one should remember that a large number of households in India face exclusion from both formal and informal credit market. Our model tried to find out the socio- economic and cultural reasons behind this.

The last model displayed the factors inducing an individual to avail a loan from informal financial markets, particularly moneylenders, who generally charge usurious interest rate. Given that the dependent variable is dichotomous in nature, we used a probit regression.

Probit Model

The probit model assumes that the values that the observed dichotomous dependent variable (Y) assumes (i.e. 1 or 0) depends on a continuous latent variable (Y*), which is again a linear function of independent variable (X). Accessibility to a financial service such as a bank account and accessibility to credit may depend on demand, supply and institutional factors as explanatory variables.

Demand for a particular financial service such as whether to have a bank account or to avail a loan on the first hand depends on the desire to avail such services. Secondly, it may depend on the ability to pay for it.

Desire to avail a financial service may depend on occupation and age of the respondent. Age may determine the desire to borrow or lend since a household's consumption may not vary much over lifetime, though its income may vary. The ability to avail a financial service may also depend on savings. A household with zero savings would not avail any kind of financial service.

Supply of financial service in a developing country like India may be a function of income, caste, religion and location of the household. Higher income is expected to increase access to financial service since it increases ability of a household to provide better collateral in the credit market.

Caste and religion are also crucial since supply of financial services is expected to change with change in religion and caste-based network. Given in Table 2.4 is the list of variables used in the regression along with mean and variance.

Table 2.4: Description of Variables

Variable Name	Description	Mean Value	Variance
Rural	Dummy Variable: Rural =1 , Urban = 0	0.4	0.5
Age	Age of the individual respondent	37.4	11.2
Rural income	Interaction between rural and income of the household	72072.6	132929.8
Urban income	Interaction between urban and income of the household	243037.7	358572.5
Male	Dummy Variable: Male =1 , Female = 0	0.5	0.5
No Savings	Dummy Variable for individuals with no savings	0.1	0.2
General Caste	Dummy Variable: General caste = 1 , Others = 0	0.6	0.5
Illiterate	Illiterate =1, others = 0	0.1	0.3
Hindu	Dummy variable: Hindu = 1, others = 0	0.9	0.3
Muslim	Dummy variable: Muslim = 1, others = 0	0.1	0.3
Self-employed	Dummy variable: self employed = 1, others = 0	0.2	0.4

Table 2.5 shows the expected impact of the explanatory variables in opening a bank account and access to credit.

Probit regression results of determinants of financial inclusion are shown in Tables 2.6a and 2.6b.

Dependent Variable: Bank Account =1, others = 0

Table 2.5: Variable and its Expected Sign with Dependent Variable

Variable name	Opening a bank account	Access to credit (formal)	Access to credit (informal)
Rural	Negative	Negative	Positive
Age	Negative	Positive	Positive
Rural income	Positive	Positive	Positive
Urban income	Positive	Positive	Positive
Male	Positive	Positive	Positive
No savings	Negative	Negative	Negative
General caste	Positive	Positive	Positive
Illiterate	Negative	Negative	Negative
Hindu	Positive	Positive	Positive
Muslim	Negative	Negative	Negative

Table 2.6a: Probit Regression: Results of Determinants of Financial Inclusion

Number of observations	1049
Wald chi2 (11)	197.47
Probability > chi2	0.0000
Pseudo R2	0.1992
Log pseudo likelihood	-537.09059

Results Explained

Probit regression results in Tables 2.6a and 2.6b show the significance of determinants of accessibility to financial service in terms of having a bank account. Here, the dependent variable is having a bank account which assumes value 1 if the respondent has a bank account and 0 otherwise.

The explanatory variables are gender, location of the respondents (rural-urban area), income of the respondents, their savings, their occupation, educational qualification, caste and religion. The term dF/dX refers to the probability of change in dependent variable in response to a change in any explanatory variable.

Table 2.6b: Probit Regression Results of Determinants of Financial Inclusion

Explanatory variables	Coefficient	dF/dX Changes in probability	Robust standard error	Z	P>Z
Urban income	1.95E-06	6.46E-07	3.32E-07	5.89	0
Rural income	-8.55E-07	-2.82E-07	3.91E-07	-2.19	0.029
Rural	0.0669342	0.0220088	0.1474055	0.45	0.65
Male	0.7058957	0.2293304	0.0967195	7.3	0
Age	0.0023294	0.0007698	0.0041301	0.56	0.573
No savings	-0.4307431	-0.1561506	0.1918065	-2.25	0.025
Self-employed	-0.5020884	-0.1787335	0.1146182	-4.38	0
Illiterate	-0.5230589	-0.1894364	0.1336832	-3.91	0
General caste	0.2071643	0.069659	0.092974	2.23	0.026
Muslim	-0.6594572	-0.2451941	0.2568011	-2.57	0.01
Hindu	-0.1179418	-0.0379343	0.1914367	-0.62	0.538
Constant	-0.0579885	-	0.2569178	-0.23	0.821

Out of the eleven explanatory variables mentioned in the table, eight variables such as income in an urban area, income in a rural area, being a male, no savings, self-employed, illiterate, general caste and Muslim are significant (below 10 percent).

In urban areas, income has shown a high significance in opening a bank account which implies that being in an urban area, higher the income level, greater is the probability of opening a bank account.

However, in rural areas, we observe an unanticipated result. The probability of opening a bank account is lower for the richer sections compared to that of poorer households.

In this context, one should note that in rural areas, in recent times, labourer and poorer households have opened a bank account to avail of the facility of 100 days of employment under the Mahatma Gandhi NREGA programme. This may be one of the reasons behind more number of accounts for economically weaker sections in rural areas.

The result also displays that being a male, increases the probability of opening a bank account. There are many housewives and aged females who have not opened a bank account. Often, they use the accounts of other family members which is the reason why males have more bank accounts than females.

Respondents having no savings also significantly influence opening of a bank account. Here, the relationship is inverse, which implies that people having no savings do not open a bank account.

If people save less it indicates they do not have enough money to save and therefore they do not open a bank account.

For self-employed, the probability of opening a bank account is less. Though self-employed people require more money but our findings suggest that they open lesser number of bank accounts vis-à-vis labourers and regular salaried households.

One of the reasons for this may be the implementation of MGNREGA. Under MGNREGA, mostly labour class households have opened a bank account.

On the other hand, most government employees are generally expected to have an account. Self-employed group remains excluded. As a result, the proportion of self-employed people having a bank account is less.

Being an illiterate reduces the probability of opening a bank account. Illiterate people are generally poor and unaware and therefore they have less money for opening a bank account.

Being a general caste increases the probability of opening a bank account. General caste people have better network in India than any other castes. Therefore, their accessibility to formal financial market is high.

Being a Muslim also decreases the probability of opening a bank account. The reason may be they are both socially and economically backward.

Often, they are not well informed about access to formal financial services. All these factors play a significant role in not opening a bank account.

Probit regression results of determinants for availing formal credit are shown in Tables 2.7a and 2.7b.

Table 2.7a: Probit Regression Results: Determinants of Availing Formal Credit

Number of observations	1,049
Wald chi2(8)	94.04
Probability > chi2	0.0000
Pseudo R2	0.1643
Log pseudo likelihood	-389.79618

Table 2.7b: Probit Regression Results of Determinants of Availing Formal Credit

Explanatory Variable	Coefficient	dF/dX	Robust Standard Error	Z	P>z
Rural	-0.1349294	-0.0282923	0.1731821	-0.78	0.436
Age	0.0030936	0.0006604	0.0045709	0.68	0.499
Rural income	-1.12E-07	-2.39E-08	5.69E-07	-0.2	0.844
Urban income	1.19E-06	2.55E-07	1.90E-07	6.28	0
Male	0.3521251	0.0755621	0.1021836	3.45	0.001
General caste	0.149076	0.0310444	0.1081024	1.38	0.168
Hindu	0.1165161	0.0237247	0.1433484	0.81	0.416
Illiterate	-0.4418516	-0.0777428	0.2110648	-2.09	0.036
Constant	-1.778068		0.2481144	-7.17	0
Probability at x bar	0.13				

Results Explained

Probit regression results in Tables 2.7a and 2.7b show the significance of determinants of accessibility to financial services in terms of availability of formal credit. Here, the dependent variable is access to formal credit which assumes value 1 if the respondent has borrowed from formal financial sector or 0 otherwise. The explanatory variables are location of the respondents (rural area), age of the respondents, income of the respondents, gender, educational qualification, caste and religion. The term dF/dX refers to the probability of change in dependent variable in response to a change in any explanatory variable.

Out of the eight explanatory variables mentioned in the table, there are three important variables including location, being a male, and being illiterate.

The probability of borrowing from formal financial sector is higher for richer sections of the society compared to that of poorer households. In this context, one should note that in recent periods, consumerism has increased manifold. Therefore, in order to buy newly available products in the market or to have a better life style, richer sections of the society in urban areas borrow more from the formal credit institutions.

The result also displays that being a male, increases the probability of borrowing from formal credit institutions. There are many housewives and aged females who are not eligible to take loans from the formal sector. Therefore, being a male play a significant role in borrowing from the formal sector.

Being an illiterate also decreases the probability of getting a loan from the formal financial sector. Illiterate people are generally poor and unaware of the credit facilities provided by formal institutions. Moreover, often they do not fulfil the eligibility criteria (such as, identification documents, security etc.) required for borrowing from the formal sector.

Probit regression results of determinants of availing informal credit are shown in Tables 2.8a and 2.8b.

Table 2.8a: Probit Regression Results: Determinants of Availing Informal Credit

Number of observations	1,049
Wald chi2(8)	24.2
Probability > chi2	0.0021
Pseudo R2	0.0367
Log pseudo likelihood	311.46273

Results Explained

Probit regression shown in Tables 2.8a and 2.8b show the determinants of accessibility to informal credit. Here, the dependent variable is access to informal credit which assumes value 1 if the respondent has borrowed from the informal financial sector or 0 otherwise. The explanatory variables include location of the respondents (rural area), age of the respondents, income of the respondents, gender, educational qualification, caste and religion. The term dF/dX refers to the probability of change in dependent variable in response to a change in any explanatory variable.

Table 2.8b: Probit Regression Results of Determinants of Availing Informal Credit

Explanatory Variable	Coefficient	dF/dX	Robust Standard Error	z	P>z
Rural	0.0306932	0.0047647	0.16695	0.18	0.854
Age	0.0070444	0.001088	0.004771	1.48	0.14
Rural income	4.49E-07	6.94E-08	4.60E-07	0.98	0.328
Urban income	-5.10E-07	-7.88E-08	2.91E-07	-1.75	0.08
Male	-0.0113769	-0.0017569	0.110992	-0.1	0.918
General caste	-0.1922715	-0.0309194	0.112762	-1.71	0.088
Hindu	-0.1957596	-0.0332551	0.153299	-1.28	0.202
Illiterate	0.2622276	0.0462237	0.155628	1.68	0.092
Constant	-1.295781		0.262972	-4.93	0
Probability at x bar	0.08				

Urban households with a higher economic status have lower probability of borrowing from the informal financial sector compared to poorer households. The reason may be that in urban areas, poorer households may have better linkages in the informal market compared to a richer household. For example, an employer may be willing to provide loan to his poor employee. However, one should also note that poorer households do not have accessibility from other sources.

General caste households possess a higher probability of borrowing from the informal sector compared to other castes. One of the reasons is that loans in informal market are generally provided to borrowers of the same caste. Since general caste people have better network and also they are economically better off in India than any other castes, they can avail of more loans (Jodhka, 1995).

Conclusions and Discussion

Financial inclusion requires consumers to have knowledge about the various financial products and services being offered and the working of the same. This imparting of knowledge must take place at the level of banks and other financial institutions. The banking sector needs to devise financial products to meet the diverse needs of consumers at minimum cost keeping in view adaptability to local conditions and diverse types of geographic and other socio-economic attributes.

Financial inclusion is imperative when a nation has to develop, but what is equally important is to understand the banking habits of people so that governments can make appropriate polices to speed up the process of financial inclusion and provide credit at reasonable rates. The informal sources of credit is still prevalent in number of villages as the expansion of formal credit has not been adequate so as to put an end to the supply of funds by informal lenders. When banking institutions make lending difficult the informal sector resultantly thrives.

We can, thus, conclude that access to formal credit is still a far cry for most people with low income and living in both urban and rural areas. Improving financial inclusion also means increasing access to credit as and when required.

References

Ananth, S. and Sabri, T. (2013), "Challenges to Financial Inclusion in India: The Case of Andhra Pradesh", *Economic and Political Weekly*, XLVII(07).

Brown, E., Castañeda, F., Cloke, J. and Taylor, P. (2013), "Towards Financial Geographies of the Unbanked: International Financial Markets, 'Bancarizacion' and Access to Financial Services in Latin America", *The Geographical Journal*, 179(3), 198-210.

Chase. S., Gjertson Leah and Collins Michael (2011), "Coming Up With Cash in a Pinch: Emergency Savings and its Alternatives", CFS Issue Brief 6, available at: http://www.cfs.wisc.edu/briefs/chasegjertsoncollins2011_cashpaper.pdf.

Chattopadhyay, S.K. (2011), "Financial Inclusion in India: A Case Study of West Bengal", Department of Economic and Policy Research, Reserve Bank of India, available at: http://www.rbi.org.in/scripts/publicationsview.Aspx?Id=13517.

Goldsmith, Raymond, W. (1969), "Financial Structure and Development", New Haven, CT: Yale University Press.

Lucas, R.E. (1998), "On The Mechanics of Economic Development", Econometric Society Monographs, 29, 61-70.

Mowl, A.J. (2012), "The Role of Transaction Costs in Access to Savings and Credit", prepared by NSE Working Paper Series, available at: http://www.nseindia.com/research/content/NSE-IFMR_Paper_1.pdf.

Patrick, H.T. (1966), "Financial Development and Economic Growth in Underdeveloped Countries", Economic Development and Cultural Change, 174-189, available at: http://www.jstor.org/discover/10.2307/1152568?uid=2&uid=4&sid=21104620508433.

Rajan, R.G. and Zingales, L. (2003), "Saving Capitalism from Capitalists", Crown Business, New York.

Romer, Paul M. (1986), "Increasing Returns and Long-Run Growth", *The Journal of Political Economy,* 1002-37, available at: http://www.jstor.org/discover/10.2307/1833190?uid=2&uid=4&sid=21104620508433.

Sparreboom, P. and Duflos, E. (2012), "Financial Inclusion in the People's Republic of China", available at: http://www.278elwb02.blackmesh.com/sites/default/files/CGAP-WMFG-Financial-Inclusion-in-China-Aug-2012.pdf.

Schumpeter, Joseph A. (1934), "The Theory of Economic Development", translated by R. Opie, Harvard University Press, Cambridge, MA.

Triki, T. and Faye, I. (2013), "Financial Inclusion in Africa: The Transformative Role of Technology", in T. Triki and I. Faye (eds.), 'Financial Inclusion in Africa', AFDB.

3

Financial Literacy of Economically Marginalized People

Abdul Azeez N.P. and Nasira Banu M.

Introduction

Access to finance, especially by the poor and vulnerable groups is a pre-requisite for getting employment, economic growth, poverty reduction and social cohesion. It will also empower the vulnerable groups by giving them an opportunity to have a bank account, to save and invest, to ensure their homes or to partake in credit, thereby facilitating them to break the chain of poverty. A well developed financial system brings poor people into the mainstream of the economy and allows them to contribute more actively to their personal economic development (Serrao, Sequeira and Basil Hans, 2012). In order to flourish and realize their potential, people need enough opportunity to participate in almost all spheres of life. But certain groups in the society suffer financially as well as socially through exclusion.

Economic marginalisation is a process that relates to an economic structure and in particular to the structure of the financial markets and their integration. To the extent that from the financial market, some individuals or groups are segmented in general, these individuals or groups can be said to be economically marginalised from the rest of the economy. This segregation results in the exclusion of the group from the financial markets. The economic behaviour of the marginalised group is distinctly different from the dominating group or elite group. Marginalised people in India can be divided into two main categories: traditionally marginalised and those marginalised in the wake and as a result of capitalist transformation. Marginalised people are those sections of the society who are economically and socially depressed and alienated from the mainstream.

According to Prahalad, C.K. (2010), these people constitute the 'bottom of the pyramid' and could be a source of much needed vitality and growth. They represent extreme variety in their levels of literacy, rural-urban mix, geographical mix, income levels, cultural and religious differences and every other conceivable basis of segmentation. These people have to mobilize, spend, save and invest money to escape from poverty. They are to be streamlined into the main flow of the nation which is one of the objectives of financial inclusion.

The concept of financial literacy means a combination of financial awareness, knowledge, skills, attitude and behaviours necessary to make sound financial decisions and ultimately achieve individual financial well-being. A number of definitions of financial literacy exist in the literature. Basically, 'financial literacy' refers to the knowledge and understanding of financial concepts thereby resulting in the ability to make informed, confident and effective decisions regarding money. In a broader perspective, financial literacy can be stated as "understanding of economics and how economic conditions and circumstances affect household decisions" (Worthington, 2006). A narrow definition of financial literacy focuses on "basic money management tools such as budgeting, savings, investing and insurance" (Natalie, Newton and Chrisann, 2010). It is the narrow view of financial literacy that is particularly relevant to individual decisions concerning financial matters.

Financial literacy of the poor or marginalised is a powerful tool for achieving the objectives of helping them to come out of the vicious cycle of poverty, as it aims at changing their attitude towards managing both money and their life, building sustainable financial knowledge and skills. Financial literacy movement aims at bringing financial independence and prosperity in the lives of people by helping them to effectively manage their earnings. It helps the poor to follow a financial strategy which enables them to build capital and assets, and eventually come out of the debt trap. This ultimately leads to financial empowerment which enables them to live happily.

Components of Financial Literacy

Financial literacy has three distinct but dependent components:

1. Core competency,
2. Proficiency, and
3. Opportunity.

A financially literate person must be proficient in core competencies and be given the opportunity and environment to acquire financial literacy and its benefits.

Core Competencies: Based on the review of literature, a financially literate person should be proficient in the following core competencies.

- Numerical ability.
- Budgeting, including the ability to keep track of expenses and income.
- Savings.
- Borrowing.
- Investment.

The core competencies are applicable to all sections of the society irrespective of socio-economic or regional considerations and can be expanded or refined, depending on the magnitude of spending, saving, borrowing and investment.

***Numerical Ability*:** Numerical ability or basics of money relates to the knowledge required for the most essential day to day calculations involving finance. This takes the form of basic calculations connected with the cost of purchasing goods, paying bills, interest and discount calculations etc. At the basic level, it is addition, multiplication, subtraction and division. Lack of numerical skills will certainly affect financial literacy. At a higher level, it is the ability to understand financial statements or other accounting information, time value of money, risk analysis etc.

Budgeting and Living Within Means: Budgeting means keeping track of finances and reducing unnecessary spending. Living within one's own means is a skill necessary for effective budgeting, and budgeting is essential when there is limited income (MAS, 2005).

Savings: Savings relate to setting aside some money for future use. It may be either short-term savings or long-term savings. While short-term savings relate to budgeting, long-term savings are relevant to post-retirement life or for purchase of costly items required in life such as a house or a car or even for marriage expenses of children.

Borrowing: In modern era, borrowing is a way of life for all categories of people. Many people take up loans or mortgages. An indicator of competent borrowing is that loan amount should be relative to earnings. A large proportion of respondents in various financial literacy surveys did not understand the difference between an unsecured or secured personal loan, and fixed or variable interest rate. Debt literacy determines proficient borrowing. The core competency of a financially literate person is the ability to understand debt, and the processes involved to avoid it, reduce it and repay it. It also relates to competence in using loans (Lusardi and Tufano, 2009) and responses to debt including the ability to determine whether debt is justified or not (World Bank, 2008). Debt illiteracy is therefore related with over-indebtedness, and an inability to reduce existing levels of debt (Lusardi and Tufano, 2009).

Investing: Competence in investing and choosing the most suitable investment portfolio is another key feature of financial literacy. Selection of an investment portfolio depends on the finance available for investment and the purpose of investment. Investment may be in real assets or financial assets. A Japanese survey suggests three criteria for choosing investments: safety, liquidity and profitability (Hiroshi, 2002).

Proficiency: All the five core competencies described above are essential for financial literacy, but these competencies also require a degree of proficiency. Thus, a financially literate person must be proficient in the core competencies, having proficient financial knowledge, ability, skill and experience in the core competencies supported by positive attitudes about money.

Financial Knowledge: An important aspect of proficiency is the level of financial knowledge of the people. This refers to a person's level of knowledge of the core competencies and the conviction that financial knowledge will lead to financial well-being.

Application of Knowledge: Definitions of financial literacy in United States (PACFL, 2008), Canada (Task Force on Financial Literacy, 2010), United Kingdom (FSA, 2011), and Australia (Financial Literacy Foundation, Australia, 2008) signify the importance of application of financial knowledge in financial literacy. The UK Treasury has stated that financially capable consumers plan ahead, find and use information, know when to seek advice and can understand and act on this advice, leading to a greater participation in the financial services market (HM Treasury, 2007). However, knowledge cannot be usefully applied without relevant skills.

Skill and Confidence: A financially capable person possesses all the skills necessary to effectively manage finances to achieve well-being, and this includes communication skills, interpersonal skills, reading skills, mathematical and computational skills etc. The definition of financial literacy adopted in the United States by the Jumpstart Coalition is "the ability to use knowledge and skills to manage financial resources effectively for a lifetime of financial well-being". The element of confidence is added by the Canadian definition of financial literacy also together with skills. "Financial literacy means having the knowledge, skills and confidence to make responsible financial decisions" (Sandra Huston, 2010). Remund in his search for a better definition of financial literacy states, "based upon a review of research studies since 2000, the many conceptual definitions of financial literacy fall into five categories: (i) knowledge of financial concepts, (ii) ability to communicate about financial concepts, (iii) aptitude in managing personal finances, (iv) skill in making appropriate financial decisions and (v) confidence in planning effectively for future financial needs" (Remund, 2010). Financial literacy therefore requires communication skills also. It includes the ability to apply knowledge and to communicate that knowledge, making financial literacy vital to effective decision-making.

Attitude and Motivation: Financial literacy is understood by the link from knowledge (Fox, 2005) to skills, to attitudes, to behaviour (Holzmann, 2010). This link is important, because knowledge influences attitudes, which then manifests into particular types of behaviour (ANZ Bank, 2008). Attitudes include whether people live for today or for the future, or whether insurance is necessary or there are preferences for risk etc. (Financial Literacy Foundation, Australia, 2008).

Rationale of the Study

Indian households make many financial decisions each year. These relate to a wide range of financial matters, including decisions on how to budget, how much to spend and to save, where to invest their money i.e., their earnings, how to manage their financial risks, how much debt they may need to fund their expenditure, and what form of debt they should take. These decisions range in complexity, but all require at least a basic level of financial literacy. In the world of escalating financial complexity, there is an increasing need for financial knowledge and at least basic financial skills. Technological advances have dramatically transformed the provision of financial services in India and around the world. There is an ever increasing diversity of financial products and services, including debt products and investment opportunities available. While this provides increased benefits, it also entails more complex risks, including risks that are not always readily apparent to the unwary. Accordingly, the scope and complexity of the financial decisions an individual has to make in managing their financial affairs has grown significantly. Individuals must be able to differentiate between a wide range of financial products and services, and providers of those products and services.

Financial literacy and financial inclusion are twin pillars where financial inclusion acts as a supply side of proving financial services and financial literacy acts as a demand side of making people acquainted with what they should buy. As the main motto of financial inclusion is to provide access to financial services to the masses at an affordable cost, it is imminent that the masses be financially literate to avail of greater benefits and augment the process of inclusive growth. Financial inclusion mainly aims at providing basic financial services and also ancillary financial services like insurance, mutual funds etc., which can only be done by improving financial literacy. Thus, financial literacy stimulates the demand side i.e. making people aware of what they can and should demand. Financial inclusion acts from the supply side, i.e. providing in the financial market what people demand.

Kerala has long been of interest to development researchers as its level of social development is much higher than that of its economic development. It is characterised by high literacy rate, low birth rate, high life expectancy and an even sex balance and ranks top among the fifteen biggest states in India on the human development index. Kerala is top among the states in financial inclusion endowed with an entrenched culture of banking, high literacy rate, significant inflow of remittances from overseas, and a widespread welfare transfer programme. Kerala has emerged as a front runner in the drive towards achieving financial inclusion since the mid-2000s. Kerala was recently declared 100 percent financially included in terms of coverage of all households with at least one bank account.

Although all the households have a bank account, they are unaware about the financial services, products and investment provisions, and possess less financial knowledge, and unsatisfactory and negative financial behaviour and attitudes. They have opened bank accounts unwillingly just to draw MGNREGA wages, old age and agricultural pensions, getting LPG and other subsidies etc. Many of them are unfamiliar with even the most basic economic concepts needed to make sensible saving and investment decisions. This has serious implications for saving, retirement planning and other financial decisions. All these lead to financial illiteracy among the people. Their knowledge about various financial institutions, financial activities and financial products is not adequate. By educating them in this regard, the economic activities will be more fruitful. Thus, financial literacy is a prerequisite for an effective financial inclusion.

Objectives of the Study

- To understand the initiative taken by various authorities to promote financial literacy;
- To analyse the determinants of financial literacy of the marginalized people of Malappuram District;
- To measure the overall financial literacy of marginalized people of Malappuram District; and
- To suggest measures to improve financial literacy of the marginalized people.

Hypotheses of the Study

The hypotheses of the study is based on the concept that financial literacy of an individual is the function of his/her financial knowledge and action over the four tiers of financial literacy, i.e. saving literacy, spending literacy, borrowing literacy and investment literacy.

The research study is designed on the basis of the following hypotheses:

H_1: Marginalized people are financially illiterate.

H_1: Financial literacy of the marginalized people is not determined by any factors.

Methodology and Sources of Data

Both types of data i.e., primary and secondary, have been collected for the purpose of study. The primary data was collected through interview schedules and focused group discussions (FGDs). Both kinds of information viz., quantitative and qualitative were gathered in order to supplement the information. The tools were developed and finalized after several rounds of interaction with a few informants and office bearers of self-help groups, banking officials and non-banking finance companies and social activists of NGOs. Before administering the interview schedule to the sample population, a pre-test was conducted to check the reliability. Secondary data was collected from various reports, periodicals and orders of the RBI and other banking and non-banking financial institutions.

For measuring the factors determining the basic financial literacy of the marginalized people, logistic regression analysis was used. In this model, estimation was made to understand the determinants of knowledge about basic financial literacy in the form of:

$$Y = a_0 + a_1X_1 + a_2X_2 + a_3X_3 + a_4X_4 \ldots\ldots\ldots\ldots\ldots\ldots + a_{17}X_{17} + u$$

Where, Y is a dependent variable—whether respondents are financial literate or not.

The challenge was to understand the importance of financial literacy and its measurement. There is no standardized measure for financial literacy. For the purpose of this study, a model was developed to measure the overall financial literacy which is outlined below:

Financial literacy = Saving literacy + Spending literacy + Borrowing literacy + Investment literacy

Accordingly, a scale was constructed (Table 3.1).

For the purpose of the study, Malappuram (District of Kerala) was divided into various block panchayats and eight blocks were selected on the basis of geographical location. From each blocks two panchayats were selected randomly and from each panchayat, 25 respondents were selected randomly, as depicted in Table 3.2.

Table: 3.1: Scale Descriptions

Levels	Scale	Descriptions
Level 1	Poor financial literacy	Respondents who have no saving or spending or borrowing or investment in any of the given formal sources. They are the financially excluded group
Level 2	Satisfactory financial literacy	Respondents who have either saving or spending or borrowing or investment in any one of the given formal sources
Level 3	Good financial literacy	Respondents who have either saving or spending or borrowing or investment in any two of the given formal sources
Level 4	Excellent financial literacy	Respondents who have saving or spending or borrowing or investment in three or more of the given formal sources

Table 3.2: Sample Framework

Block panchyat	Gram panchayat	Number of respondents
Malappuram	Morayur	25
	Anakkayam	25
Tirur	Vettom	25
	Tirunavaya	25
Ponnani	Edappal	25
	Kaladi	25
Kalikavu	Kalikavu	25
	Thuvvoor	25
Nilambur	Edakkara	25
	Karulai	25

Contd...

Kondotty	Vazhayur	25
	Vazhakkad	25
Perinthalmanna	Elamkulam	25
	Melattur	25
Vengara	AR Nagar	25
	Edarikkode	25
8	**16**	**400**

Determinants of Basic Financial Literacy

Determinants of basic financial literacy focused more sharply on the respondent's knowledge of basic financial literacy and for this purpose ordinary least square (OLS) regression model was used. The full model regression was fitted with seventeen independent variables.

This model determines how various independent variables, namely, age of the head of the household, gender, income, expenditure, total monthly income of the family, monthly income earned by respondents, monthly income contributed by family members, borrowing, fixed expenditure, variable expenditure, discretionary expenditure, tenure of housing, family size, number of earning members, amount of saving, financial liabilities, mode of saving, regularity of saving and participation in financial inclusion significantly influence the knowledge of basic financial literacy of the respondents (Table 3.3).

Table 3.3: Determinants of Financial Literacy

Independent Variables	UC		SC	t	Sig. (p-value)
	B	Std. Error	Beta		
Constant	253.671	32.347	0.28	.2148433	0.30
Age	-2.3456	2.459	-0.027	-.5160534	0.23
Gender	8.37814	5.368	0.065	.00568939	0.193
Marital status	-12.452	7.473	-0.078	-.0081009	0.040
Educational qualifications	-7.3412	5.729	-0.003	-.008443	0.34

Contd...

Occupation	4.2341	4.550	0.035	.5629262	0.213
Income	2.1001	1.047	0.054	.0404409	0.231
Fixed expenditure	-0.728	0.014	-0.023	-.4837774	0.410
Discretionary exp.	3.2121	0.365	0.079	.9722301	0.5792
Amount of saving	-2.341	1.0352	-0.0564	-1.2405	0.059
Mode of saving	6.5322	6.763	0.076	.14147	0.831
Regularity of saving	0.8554	1.549	0.045	3.1975	0.321
Welfare benefit received	11.908	6.36	0.073	2.1614	0.513
Financial liabilities	4.206	2.485	0.0234	.93272	0.102
Number of earning members	-4.367	4.0784	-0.0829	-1.1163	0.432
Tenure of housing	1.8760	4.465	0.057	.34672	0.115
Family size	1.3982	14.560	0.367	.65159	0.2403
Participation in financial inclusion	3.7265	3.586	0.068	.89905	0.1829
Number of Household= 400 R Square= 0.5760, Adjusted R Square= 0.328 F Value 5.503 Significant (P-Value)= 0.001					

UC = Unstandardized Coefficients; SC = Standardized Coefficients.

Table 3.3 depicts the effect of basic financial literacy using different independent variables in the entire study area. Out of seventeen independent variables, only eleven variables were significant at different probability levels. Low income households were characterized by low level of education and awareness and low income with, resulting in R square value of 0.5760, thereby indicating that 57.60 percent of variation was influenced by eleven significant variables regards the basic financial literacy knowledge of all the sample households taken together. The ordinary least square (OLS) regression model revealed a significant F value.

The mode of saving emerged as a highly significant explanatory variable in determination of basic financial literacy of the respondents. When the mode of savings increased by one unit the basic financial literacy increased by 6.532 units and was found significant at 1 percent level. The informal mode of saving was found to be a popular type of saving among low income households. Convenience is the factor determining the mode of saving.

The informal mode of savings like private finance, chit funds and money lenders were easily approachable than formal saving modes and since not requiring complex legal procedures, was more popular among low income households. Similar to this finding, the mode of saving and knowledge about basic financial literacy was found highly significant in the DNB Household Survey (DHS) (Annmaria Lusaria, 2008).

Regularity of saving turned out to be statistically significant at one percent level with an expected positive sign. A one percent increase in regularity of saving led to a 0.853 percent increase in basic financial literacy knowledge.

The welfare benefits received from the government resulted in a strong positive influence on basic financial literacy knowledge and turned out to be statistically significant at one percent level with an expected positive sign.

Since the welfare benefits were distributed through banking channels, the respondents were exposed to banking practice, resulting in an increase in basic financial literacy.

The financial liabilities or borrowings were found to have a strong positive influence on basic financial literacy concepts and emerged as an important explanatory variable and statistically highly significant. Higher the borrowing higher will be the knowledge on basic financial literacy. This is due to commitment to repay loans on the part of the respondents resulting in an increase in basic financial literacy.

Small family size was expected to influence basic financial literacy. Basic financial literacy would increase by 1.398 units when the family size of the respondents comprised of three members and it was significant at 1 percent level.

When a respondent's participation in financial inclusion increased by one unit, basic financial literacy increased by 3.725 units and was significant at a five percent level. The various financial inclusion programmes initiated by Government of India emerged as a highly significant variable in providing basic financial literacy among the respondents.

The occupation of the head of the household in unorganized sector displayed a positive coefficient (4.23); a higher level of occupation position results in better financial literacy. Similar results were also witnessed as regards higher level of occupation position showing a positive coefficient thereby increasing the knowledge of financial literacy (Hogarth, 2002).

Discretionary expenditure affected the basic financial literacy of the respondents and showed a positive sign. Households incurring greater discretionary expenditure did not get the opportunity to provide surplus in order to save, thereby loosing the opportunity even though gaining basic financial literacy knowledge. The amount of savings of the households affected basic financial literacy.

The analysis reveals that there is a negative relationship between the age of the head of the household and knowledge of basic financial literacy (-2.34) and it was also significant at a five percent level.

If the head of a household was of middle age—between 30 and 50 years—basic financial literacy will decrease by 2.34 units and the middle age group heads of households did not support knowledge about financial literacy.

The marital status of the head of the household does affect basic financial literacy knowledge. Marital status resulted in a negative coefficient (-12.452) and had an insignificant value with the expectation that unmarried respondents were likely to have more surplus out of their incomes to save than the married respondents and they are likely to acquire basic financial literacy knowledge as a result of this saving practice.

The educational status of the head of a household showed a negative influence with respect to basic financial literacy knowledge. When the educational status of the head of a household was up to school level, the basic financial literacy would decrease by 7.341 units and was found to be significant at one percent level.

Higher the educational attainment, higher was the basic financial literacy expected. The number of earning members in a household also affects basic financial literacy knowledge in a negative way and resulted in a statistically highly significant variable. This indicates that an increase in the number of earning members tend to increase the surplus income of the households. But contrary to the expectation, this relationship was found to be negative among low income households.

It implies that among the low income households, the tendency to spend is more than to save. It is likely due to non-exposure to various means of savings.

House ownership or otherwise affects basic financial literacy. It is expected that house ownership saves the rental charges and thereby provides a surplus to save and invest thereby influencing knowledge regards basic financial literacy. The relationship in this context was found to be significant at a five percent level.

When the house ownership of the respondents is owned, level of basic financial literacy will decrease. Fixed component of household expenditure is to be met irrespective of the income of the household.

When fixed expenditure increases, basic financial literacy is reduced by 0.784 units and was found to be significant at a ten percent level. Increase in fixed expenditure of the households hinders the opportunity of the respondents in acquiring basic financial literacy.

Gender of the head of the households does affect basic financial literacy knowledge. Male head households had a coefficient with a negative sign and were also insignificant. It was otherwise discovered that female headed households had better financial literacy in the study area.

Measurement of Financial Literacy

Financial literacy is typically an input to model the need for financial education and explain variation in financial behaviours.

An appropriate measuring of financial literacy is essential to understand the educational impact as well as barriers to effective financial choice and awareness.

To measure the levels of financial literacy and to find

means to improve it, a unique construct is required to measure consumers' ability to make effective financial decisions and management. Despite its importance, the academic literature has given little attention to measurement of financial literacy.

For the purpose of analysing financial literacy of the marginalised people, data was collected in six areas of financial literacy viz. numerical literacy, general financial awareness, saving literacy, spending literacy, borrowing literacy and investment literacy. Numerical literacy and general financial awareness were not taken into account to measure financial literacy.

All the respondents scored full in answering the questions on basic arithmetic and so this dimension was not included. Since the conceptual base of the study is financial behaviour (financial knowledge + financial action), awareness of general financial terms was not included to measure financial literacy of the marginalised people.

Numerical Literacy: Many studies on financial literacy start with questions first popularised by Annamaria Lusardi (2009) consisting of arithmetical questions related to addition, multiplication and division (Table 3.4).

Financial literacy test scores are highly correlated with arithmetic test scores suggesting that financial literacy tests may partly measure an innate or acquired ability to solve numerical problems in general.

In a study conducted by Shawn and Bilal (2009) to examine the reason for low demand for formal services in emerging markets of India and Indonesia, three numerical questions used by Lusardi and Mitchell (2006) were asked and correct answers were found in 52 percent cases in Indonesia and in 34 percent cases in India.

The ability of a poor person to count his earnings, to check the purchase bills, counting the balance cash received from a shop, calculation of simple interest on his borrowings or deposits etc. are strong indicators of financial literacy. To some people, financial literacy is arithmetical literacy.

Additions, subtractions, divisions and multiplications are basic arithmetical skills needed for an individual for easy dealings in money in daily life. Kerala is having the highest literacy rate of 93.91 percent as per the 2011 Census.

Table 3.4: Numerical Literacy

S. No	Questions	Correct answer	%
1.	You are going to a shop with ₹ 200. You buy provisions for ₹ 185. How much balance do you get?	400	100
2.	You go to a shop with ₹ 300. Boiled rice per kg. is ₹ 20. How much kg. of rice you can buy?	400	100
3.	You take a loan of ₹ 1,000 from your self-help group. You have to pay ₹ 100 per annum as interest. What is the rate of interest?	387	96.75
4.	You take a loan of ₹ 2,000 from your self-help group. You have to pay 11 weekly instalments of ₹ 200 each. How much you have to pay?	341	85.25

Measurement of Saving Literacy

Saving is the portion of disposable income not spent on consumption of consumer goods but accumulated or invested directly in some financial or real assets by an individual. Individuals are in charge of their own financial security (Annamaria Lusardi, 2008). Saving pre-supposes surplus personal income either from any occupation or profession. The amount of money needed by an individual and his family to live in this modern world is a question of fact. It can generally be stated that the level of financial literacy will be high if the income earned is effectively used for having a quality life (better living conditions, adequate savings etc.). Income from agriculture and allied activities is another source of income for the people. Marginalised people may not have substantial cultivable agricultural land. A few of them may engage in farming on lease basis.

Nowadays, self-help groups are actively engaged in joint farming under their banner and share the profit amongst them.

An individual can legitimately earn income from other sources in addition to income from salary or wages or from agriculture. Earnings from other sources depend on the mindset of the people. In case of marginalised people additional income can be earned by sale of livestock which they keep and feed at their home. They may also engage in self-employment schemes like street vending of vegetables and fish, lottery sales etc. In the case of marginalized groups, a strong financial literacy will be present if they mobilize money from sources other than the normal earnings. In the case of poor households, livestock farming is a common form of mobilizing money. Mobilizing money over and above the normal form of earnings is a strong indicator of financial literacy.

Saving literacy is measured by considering whether the respondents have savings in formal avenues rather than savings in informal avenues or keeping money at home. This is based on the premise that decision to save in formal avenues is a demonstration of core competencies and skill of the respondents. A scale was constructed to compare the literacy level based on the number of formal avenues in which the respondents have savings.

Level 1: Poor Saving Literacy—No savings in any formal avenues.

Level 2: Satisfactory Saving Literacy—Savings in any one of the given formal avenues.

Level 3: Good Saving Literacy—Savings in any two of the given formal avenues.

Level 4: Very Good Saving Literacy—Savings in any three of the given formal avenues.

Level 5: Excellent Saving Literacy—Savings in all available formal avenues.

Table 3.5 shows the level of saving literacy of the respondents.

The marginalised people of Malappuram district have a good saving literacy level (45 percent). Only 20 families out of the 400 respondents had poor saving literacy. These families were not using any formal avenues for savings.

Measurement Spending Literacy

The economic status of a society or community refers to its position as to where it stands on the ladder of financial position. The important determinants of economic status of a society are its per capita income, the standard of living, the level of consumption etc. The standard of living of a household can be understood from the consumption pattern, and the quality of domestic spending clearly indicates the level of welfare of the household.

Table 3.5: Level of Saving Literacy

S. No.	Level of Saving Literacy	Respondents	Percent over total
1.	Level 1: Poor saving	20	5
2.	Level 2: Satisfactory saving	52	13
3.	Level 3: Good saving	180	45
4.	Level 4: Very good saving	128	32
5.	Level 5: Excellent saving	20	5
	Total	400	100

Spending behaviour of the marginalised people has a unique pattern. Field study by the researcher revealed that poor people cannot afford costly consumer items or household equipments. The houses are electrified and most of the respondents have televisions and few respondents have computer system. Mobile phones and landline phone are popular among them. For buying household general provisions, they prefer public distribution system, and nearby local shops. The study mainly focus on monitoring of domestic expenditure, reasons for not planning expenditure, hospitalisation needs and the use of subsidised price shops for buying household items.

Spending literacy measures the willingness of the marginalised people to use subsidised price facilities offered by the Government in the presence of lower income and the resultant lower purchasing power. Spending literacy of the respondents is measured by considering the ability and willingness to use subsidised price facilities for the purchase of household items where there is possibility of savings. Many sources of purchase are available for the marginalised people, e.g., public distribution shops, subsidised prices stores (Maveli store, Supplyco, Neethi store etc.). For constructing a scale for measuring spending literacy, the purchasing behaviour of the respondents was considered; whether they are actually using money saving sources for purchase of household items. Purchase from local shops was not considered as the price of household items will be comparatively higher in these shops in relation to subsidised price shops and at the same time it was common source of purchase for all people. The scale for measuring spending literacy was follows:

Level 1: Poor spending literacy—No use of any money saving sources.

Level 2: Satisfactory spending literacy—Use of any one of the given formal sources.

Level 3: Good spending literacy—Use of any two of the given four formal sources.

Level 4: Very good spending literacy—Use of any three of the given four formal sources.

Level 5: Excellent spending literacy—Use of all the given four formal sources.

Table 3.6 shows the level of spending literacy of the respondents.

Table 3.6: Level of Spending Literacy

S. No.	Level of spending literacy	Respondents	Percent over total
1.	Level 1: Poor spending	12	3
2.	Level 2: Satisfactory spending	32	8
3.	Level 3: Good spending	260	65
4.	Level 4: Very good spending	72	18
5.	Level 5: Excellent spending	24	6
	Total	400	100

3 percent of the respondents had Level 1 spending literacy, i.e. these respondents were using only local shops for purchasing daily needs of provisions. 8 percent of the respondents came under Level 2 category, 65 percent came under Level 3 category, 18 percent came under Level 4 category and only 6 percent came under Level 5 category. Majority of the respondents had an optimum combination of all the facilities available to meet their daily needs of consumable items.

Measurement of Borrowing Literacy

Borrowing money involves obligation to return the sums borrowed as per the terms and conditions expressly or impliedly stated at the time of borrowing. Always borrowing of money or availing of credit facility is costly in the form of interest on repayment. The borrower has to pay interest on the borrowed sums as fixed by the lender at the time of borrowing along with the principal amount. People or households borrow when they are not able to meet both the ends, i.e., income and spending are unequal. Borrowing is opted when personal or household expenses exceed the money mobilized or income earned. This is true in case of individuals, institutions and even countries.

Borrowing literacy of the respondents was measured by examining whether the respondents used formal sources for meeting their financial needs. The formal sources of borrowing are commercial banks, co-operative banks, self-help groups, local bodies etc. Availing loan from private money lenders was not considered for measuring borrowing literacy.

Level 1: Below average borrowing literacy—No use of given formal sources.

Level 2: Satisfactory borrowing literacy— Use of any one of the four given formal sources.

Level 3: Good borrowing literacy—Use of any two of the four given formal sources.

Level 4: Very good borrowing literacy—Use of any three of the four given formal sources.

Level 5: Excellent borrowing literacy—-Uses of all the four given formal sources.

Borrowing literacy level of the respondents measures the use of formal sources by the marginalised people for meeting their financial needs. Many factors influence the selection of sources. Table 3.7 shows the borrowing literacy level of the respondents.

Table 3.7: Level of Borrowing Literacy

S. No.	Level of borrowing literacy	Respondents	Percent over total
1.	Level 1: Poor borrowing	20	5
2.	Level 2: Satisfactory borrowing	68	17
3.	Level 3: Good borrowing	172	43
4.	Level 4: Very good borrowing	96	24
5.	Level 5: Excellent borrowing	44	11
	Total	400	100

Among the respondents, 5 percent had Level 1 borrowing literacy, 17 percent had Level 2 borrowing literacy, 43 percent had Level 3 borrowing literacy, 24 percent had level 4 borrowing literacy and only 11 percent had a Level 5 borrowing literacy.

Measurement of Investment Literacy

Investment in a broader sense means putting money into something with the expectation of gain that upon thorough analysis has a high degree of security for the principal amount, as well as security of return, within an expected period of time. Investment is related to saving or deferring consumption. The surplus money with an individual may be deposited in a bank or in some other areas depending on the perception of the investor.

Whatever decision is made, investment means a sacrifice in the present in the hope of deriving benefits in the future. Every investment decision has two key aspects: time and risk.

While the sacrifice occurs in the present and is certain, the benefits come in the future and may be uncertain. The economic well-being of a person in the long-run depends significantly on how wisely an investment decision is made.

To measure investment literacy, eight formal investment avenues generally available to the people were selected and included in the questionnaire. A scale was constructed to compare the literacy level based on the number of formal avenues in which the respondents invest. Keeping cash at home was not considered as an indicator of financial literacy.

Level 1: Poor investment literacy—Not using any given formal avenues.

Level 2: Satisfactory investment literacy—Using any one of the four given formal avenues.

Level 3: Good investment literacy—Using any two of the four given formal avenues.

Level 4: Very good investment literacy—Using any three of the given formal avenues.

Level 5: Excellent investment literacy—Using more than three given formal avenues.

Table 3.8 shows the level of investment literacy of the respondents.

- 19 percent of the respondents had a Level 1 investment literacy, i.e. they had no investments in approved avenues.
- 2.32 percent of the respondents had a Level 2 investment literacy, i.e. they had investments in one formal investment avenue.
- 29 percent of the respondents had a Level 3 investment literacy, i.e. they had investments in two formal investment avenues.
- 4.16 percent of the respondents had a Level 4 investment literacy, i.e. they had investments in three formal investment avenues.
- 5.4 percent of the respondents had a Level 5 investment literacy, i.e. they had investments in more than three formal investment avenues.

Table 3.8: Level of Investment Literacy

S. No.	Level of investment literacy	Respondents	Percent over total
1.	Level 1: Below average investment literacy	76	19
2.	Level 2: Satisfactory investment literacy	128	32
3.	Level 3: Good investment literacy	116	29
4.	Level 4: Very good investment literacy	64	16
5.	Level 5: Excellent investment literacy	16	4
	Total	400	100

Measurement of Overall Financial Literacy

Overall financial literacy is the aggregate of the four tiers of financial literacy i.e. saving literacy, spending literacy, borrowing literacy and investment literacy.

Overall financial literacy = saving literacy + spending literacy + borrowing literacy + investment literacy.

Analysis of the overall financial literacy level of the respondents reveals the following (Table 3.9).

Table 3.9: Overall Financial Literacy

S. No.	Level of financial literacy	Respondents	Percent over total
1.	Level 1: Poor financial literacy	76	19
2.	Level 2: Satisfactory financial literacy	128	32
3.	Level 3: Good financial literacy	116	29
4.	Level 4: Excellent financial literacy	64	16
	Total	400	100

- 19 percent respondents had a Level 1 financial literacy, i.e. out of the total respondents, 19 respondents used no formal sources for savings, spending, borrowing or investment. They were totally excluded from the mainstream formal financial system.
- 32 percent respondents had a Level 2 financial literacy, i.e. out of the total respondents, 32 respondents used one of the given formal sources either for savings, spending, borrowing or investment.
- 29 of the respondents had a Level 3 financial literacy, i.e. out of total respondents, 29 respondents used any two of the given formal sources either for savings, spending, borrowing and investment.
- 16 percent of the respondents had a Level 4 financial literacy, i.e. out of the total respondents, 16 respondents used three or more of the given formal sources either for savings, spending, borrowing and investment.

Financial literacy is one of the essential requirements for achieving personal well-being as well as well-being of the members in the family. A financially literate person should be proficient in core competencies like basics of money, savings, spending, borrowing and investment. Marginalized people are those sections of the society with limited means. They must learn how to live within their means.

The analysis of primary data collected through sample survey reveals that a majority of marginalised people (81 percent) were living within their means and had knowledge and use of all the formal financial sources. Their attitude towards money management was positive.

Financial Literacy Initiatives in India

Like never before, researchers, public authorities, community groups, industrial associations and international organisations are developing financial literacy initiatives to help people become financially literate, i.e., to have the knowledge, understanding, skills and competence to deal with everyday financial matters and make right choices for their needs. Financial literacy and awareness clearly promotes economic growth and well-being by expanding the quality of available financial services, and by enhancing the ability of individuals to more effectively use these services for their best interest.

There are seven broad areas of concern that call for enhanced financial education and financial literacy initiatives all over the world.

1. There is a rapid and growing sophistication of financial markets, as a result of deregulation, globalisation and technological progress in the financial marketplace. Consumers are now faced with a variety of complex financial instruments offering a large range of options.
2. Households now assume more of a responsibility and risk for financial decisions in the context of inclination towards more liberalised economies all over the world.
3. Rapid developments in several emerging economies have resulted in the explosion of financial products being offered to a vast number of new consumers and many of whom have only limited experience with formal financial systems.
4. Inclusive growth policy all over the world aiming at inclusion of the poor and marginalised community in the mainstream of formal financial network.
5. Today, employment trends are changing such that fewer people have long-term, continuous employment. Part-time, contract, and non-permanent employment requires a different set of financial management skills than those needed by full-time permanent employees.
6. Surveys indicate that many people do not have an adequate financial background for understanding the financial matters. The OECD Survey (Improving Financial Literacy: Analysis of Issues and Policies) found that financial understanding is low among consumers across OECD countries, especially among the less educated, minorities,

and those at the lower end of the income distribution.

7. Improving financial literacy benefits at all levels of the economy and supporting the financial services sector.

Initiatives by Reserve Bank of India (RBI)

The importance of financial literacy in India is clear from the speech delivered by Dr. D. Subbarao in a RBI-OECD workshop on Financial Literacy. "In the Reserve Bank, we treat financial inclusion and financial literacy as twin pillars. Financial literacy stimulates the demand side—making people aware of what they can and should demand. Financial inclusion acts from the supply side providing in the financial market what people demand. While we have traditionally focused more on addressing financial exclusion through many supply-side measures so as to help "connect people" with the banking system, we have come to recognize the demand side imperative also—that financial literacy and education should be developed hand in hand with improving access to financial services".

In India, the need for financial literacy is even greater considering the low levels of literacy and a large section of the population, which is still left out of the formal financial set up. Towards this end, the Reserve Bank of India has undertaken a project titled "Project Financial Literacy". The objective of the project is to disseminate information regarding the Reserve Bank and general banking concepts to various target groups, including, school and college going children, women, rural and urban poor, defence personnel and senior citizens. The project envisages a multi-pronged approach.

The project is implemented in two modules: one module in which 'Money Kumar' familiarises with the role and functions of the Reserve Bank of India; and through the other module, 'Raju' which introduces the banking concepts. The material is created in English, Hindi, and regional languages. It is disseminated to the target audience with the help, among others, of banks, local government machinery, schools and colleges through presentations, pamphlets, brochures, films, as also, through the Bank's website.

In India, financial literacy initiatives are linked to Financial Inclusion Programmes which is a joint initiative of all commercial banks with the support of RBI and NABARD. In 2006-07, the RBI announced a drive for 'Financial Inclusion' that would be initiated in every state, whereby the State Level Banking Committees (SLBC) and the state lead banks would be responsible for promoting 100 percent financial inclusion in at least one district in their home states. The SLBC is a committee, consisting of representatives from all banks in a state, the state government, and the RBI, that meets regularly to coordinate state banking activities. The lead bank in a state is the bank with the most number of branches, and hence, outreach in the state. The lead bank is also the Convener of the SLBC.

The Finance Minister in his Budget Speech 2010-11 stated: "to reach the benefits of banking services to the 'Aam Aadmi', the Reserve Bank of India had set up a High Level committee on the Lead Bank Scheme. After careful assessment of the recommendations of this Committee, and in further consultation with RBI, it has been decided to provide appropriate banking facilities to habitations having population in excess of 2,000 by March 2012. It is also proposed to extend insurance and other services to the targeted beneficiaries. These services will be provided using the business correspondent and other models with appropriate technology back up. By this arrangement, it is proposed to cover 60,000 habitations".

Accordingly, the banks through the forum of State Level Banker Committees (SLBCs) have formulated their roadmaps for financial inclusion and have identified approximately 73,000 habitations having a population of over 2,000 for providing banking facilities. These habitations have been allocated to commercial banks, regional rural banks and cooperatives banks for providing banking facilities in a time bound manner. This is estimated to provide new bank accounts to around 5 crore rural households. The Financial Inclusion Campaign "Swabhimaan" was formally launched on 10th February, 2011. "Swabhimaan" aims at providing branchless banking through use of technology. Banks will provide basic services like deposits, withdrawals and remittances using the services of business correspondents (*Bank Saathi*).

The initiative enables Government subsidies and social security benefits to be directly credited to the accounts of the beneficiaries and who would be able to draw the money from the business correspondents in their village itself. Several other initiatives have also been taken by the Government of India and the RBI for furthering the reach of banking services and financial inclusion as under:

Simplified Branch Authorisation: RBI has permitted domestic scheduled commercial banks to freely open branches with population of less than 50,000 under general permission, subject to reporting. RBI has advised banks that while preparing their Annual Branch Expansion Plan (ABEP), banks should allocate at least 25 percent of the total number of branches proposed to be opened during a year in unbanked rural centres.

Relaxed KYC Norms: The know your customer (KYC) requirements for opening bank accounts have been relaxed and simplified for accounts with balances not exceeding ₹ 50,000 and aggregate credits in the accounts not exceeding ₹ 1 lakh a year.

No-frills Accounts: Reserve Bank of India, advised all scheduled commercial banks to make available a basic 'no-frills' account with 'nil' or very low minimum balances that would make such accounts accessible to vast sections of the population.

General Credit Cards: A general purpose credit card (GCC) facility up to ₹ 25,000 has been provided by the banks at their rural and semi-urban branches.

Business Correspondents (BCs): The scope of entities eligible to be engaged as business correspondents by the banks has been enlarged by RBI from time to time. In April 2010, the RBI permitted banks to engage any individuals as BCs by banks. Recently RBI permitted "for-profit" corporate entities to be engaged as BCs. The BC model allows banks to do 'cash in-cash out' transactions at a location much closer to the rural population, thus addressing the last mile problem.

Core Banking Solutions in RRBs: The Reserve Bank of India has directed the sponsor banks of regional rural banks (RRBs) to speedily, and fully, implement core banking solution (CBS) in all RRBs and commit to firm timeline by September 2011, by which all RRBs will become fully CBS compliant. This is expected to give a further fillip to financial inclusion efforts given the penetrative outreach of the RRBs in the rural areas.

Mobile Banking: The Reserve Bank of India issued the guidelines for mobile banking transactions in October 2008. The guidelines permit banks to provide mobile banking transactions and mandates that all transactions have to originate from one bank account and terminate in another bank account.

Special Package for North-Eastern States: To improve banking penetration in the North-East, the Reserve Bank asked the State Governments in the region and banks to identify centres where there is a need for setting up either full-fledged branches or those offering for ex-facilities, handling government business or for meeting currency requirements. There also exists a viability gap funding scheme of providing financial support to banks by the Reserve Bank for setting up banking facilities viz., currency chests, extension of foreign exchange and Government business facilities at "agreed" centres in the North-Eastern Region, which are not found to be economically viable by banks. The scheme requires the State Governments to make available necessary premises and other institutional support.

FIF and FITF: Based on the recommendations of the "Committee on Financial Inclusion" set up by the Government of India under Dr. C. Rangarajan, two funds, namely the "Financial Inclusion Fund (FIF)" for meeting the cost of developmental and promotional interventions for ensuring financial inclusion, and the "Financial Inclusion Technology

Fund (FITF)", to meet the cost of technology adoption has been set up at NABARD with an overall corpus of ₹ 500 crore each. The corpus is shared by GoI, RBI and NABARD in the ratio of 40:40:20.

Financial Literacy and Credit Counselling Centres: Each SLBC convenor has been asked to set up a credit-counselling centre in one district as a pilot, and extend it to all other districts in due course. As in March 2011, banks have reported setting up 225 credit counselling centres in various States of the country. A model scheme on Financial Literacy and Credit Counselling Centres (FLCCs) was formulated and communicated to all scheduled commercial banks and RRBs with the advice to set up the centres as distinct entities maintaining an arm's length from the bank so that the FLCC's services are available to even other banks' customers in the district.

SHG-Bank Linkage Programme: To give an impetus to micro finance, the same was categorized under priority sector lending and lending to SHGs was brought under the weaker sections of the priority sector. Banks have been advised to provide adequate incentives to their branches for financing the SHGs.

Financial Literacy and Credit Counselling Centres (FLCCs): The Reserve Bank of India directed all scheduled commercial banks including RRBs to initiate Financial Literacy and Credit Counselling Centres (FLCC) from 2008 onwards with the broad objective of providing free financial literacy/education and credit counselling. While the FLCCs centres would provide financial literacy and credit counselling, the activities of the Rural Development and Self-Employed Training Institutes (RUDSETI) towards skill development and capacity building could be dovetailed with FLCCs initiatives, for increasing the earnings/debt repaying ability of the distressed borrowers' families' allied activities. Indian Institute for Development and Research in Banking Technology (IDRBT) was created by RBI in 1996 in order to develop easier access to financial services for vulnerable groups.

The main purpose of the Institute is to promote use of technology in the banking sector and identify and develop information technology to overcome financial exclusion in India and especially in small villages spread over the country. IDBRT is fighting for financial inclusion and in particular the development of common standards for the use of technology and innovative financial services such as smartcards, micro ATMs and mobile banking. Stressing the necessity of financial literacy among people in India, The Reserve Bank of India has been very eager to include financial courses at both schools and colleges in different states of the country. RBI's financial literacy programme is already being pursued in the state of Karnataka as a pilot study and now based on that experience, the bank plans to extend it to the state of Odisha. The financial inclusion drive of the RBI which is a part of the Platinum Jubilee celebrations of the Bank includes initiating financial awareness in all parts of India and also introduction of financial education in schools and colleges.

Initiatives Taken by Commercial Banks

Allahabad Bank: "Samadhan", the first Financial Literacy and Credit Counselling Centre, promoted by Allahabad Bank, the oldest joint stock bank of the country celebrating 145th year of its purposeful existence, was inaugurated in Kolkata. People having limited resources and skills to appreciate the complexities of financial dealings including individuals can avail the facility of financial literacy and credit counselling free of cost from the counsellors posted at this centre.

Andhra Bank: Andhra Bank has released pamphlets and deployed publicity-vans for educating the rural people on the financial inclusion scheme. The branch managers are visiting the villages to promote financial literacy for the benefit of rural people. Supervisors-on-contract basis have been appointed for promoting financial literacy in the villages. A documentary has been prepared for display in rural areas as a part of financial inclusion literacy drive. Mobile jeeps mounted with publicity material on financial literacy are also deployed in the rural areas.

Bank of Baroda: Bank of Baroda has opened Financial Literacy and Credit Counselling Centres as a CSR initiative. The centre opened is christened as "Saarthee" amply indicating its basic objective of steering those under financial distress and educating others to avoid financial mess. The bank has set up FLCCs at 45 Centres all over India.

Bank of India: Bank of India being a major bank in the public sector endeavours to strike a viable equilibrium between commercial objectives and social responsibilities. The Credit Counselling services were started under the aegis of the Trust "Abhay".

Bank of Maharashtra: The Bank has Lead Bank responsibility in six districts of Maharashtra and under 'Swabhiman', the bank has been allotted 1,215 unbanked villages in the country to be covered under financial inclusion for inclusive growth. Bank of Maharashtra has FLCCs in all the districts of Maharashtra.

Canara Bank: Canara Bank has set up Financial Literacy and Credit Counselling Centres named as "Amulya" in the states of West Bengal, Kerala, Karnataka and Bihar to impart/ disseminate knowledge to the rural poor about the objectives of financial inclusion and various banking and financial services available to them especially at their door step. The Bank has also registered a new trust, "Canara Financial Advisory Trust" to manage these Financial Literacy and Credit Counselling Centres.

Dena Bank: In pursuance with the guidelines of the RBI to set up Credit Counselling Centres, Dena Bank has named its Credit Counselling Centre as 'Dena Mitra'.

Indian Overseas Bank: IOB has a financial inclusion cell. The Bank decided to extend banking services to allotted villages through Smart Card Banking with the use of business correspondents (BCs). 'Sneha' is the Financial Literacy and Credit Counselling Centre (FLCC) established by the bank and it is the Lead Bank for Thiruvananthapuram District of Kerala.

Oriental Bank of Commerce: The Bank has opened 4 Financial Literacy and Credit Counselling (FLCC) Centres in Karnal and Palwal Districts of Haryana, Sriganganagar in Rajasthan and Ferozpur in Punjab.

Punjab and Sind Bank: Punjab and Sind Bank has entered into a tie-up with M/s HCL Info Systems Ltd. for provision of smart card based technology solution for financial inclusion besides engaging and managing business correspondents deployed in unbanked villages allotted.

Syndicate Bank: Syndicate Bank has taken various initiatives for effective implementation of the financial inclusion and financial literacy programme. Exclusive Financial Inclusion Department was formed at the corporate office headed by a general manager for constant monitoring and supervision. The Bank has opened 14 FLCCs in Karnataka under Jnana Jyotthi Financial Literacy and Credit Counselling Trust.

Union Bank of India: According to the Bank authorities, the first step towards financial inclusion should be financial literacy which is a prerequisite to make financial inclusion meaningful and sustainable. Financial literacy is to help the unreached sectors realize the importance of financial services in improving the standard of their living and where and how the services can be availed, i.e. to basically create a need and synergize the demand thus created with the supply of financial services by the formal institutions. The village knowledge centres (VKCs) and bank branches are doing well to spread financial literacy. In order to expedite the process, given its importance for the FI project, the Bank has planned opening 14 FLCCs across its 14 lead districts to begin with to fulfil its mandate of financial literacy and counselling of the unreached and unbanked sector.

State Bank of India: Keeping in tune with the GoI initiatives, State Bank of India planned its goals for stabilizing and forwarding financial inclusion efforts. The Bank restructured its administrative layers at corporate centre,

Mumbai creating rural business unit for focusing on agriculture advances, development of technological initiatives servicing the deposit and advances products, service remittance products and sell micro investment and insurance products by closely monitoring banking correspondents and creating national level alliances. Bank has already tied up with 10 national alliances including India Post, Zero MASS, ITC etc. and other 10 regional level alliances. Bank has designed and implemented the SBI Tiny Card savings bank accounts based on smart card based technology, operated with fingerprint identification.

Federal Bank: Federal Bank is providing yeoman service in the field of financial literacy and financial inclusion in Kerala. The Bank has established a trust namely "Federal Ashwas Trust". The main objective the Trust is the establishment and running of "Federal Ashwas Financial Literacy and Credit Counselling Centres" (FAFLCC) for providing financial education and credit counselling to the public. Credit counselling is being provided for existing as well as prospective customers of all banks at all the centres by the counsellors, who are retired bank employees. The counsellors visit branches of all banks in their area and spread the message of availability of Federal Ashwas Financial Literacy and Credit Counselling Centre.

Counsellors are also attending block and district level banker's committee meetings to request banks and Government departments to advise the public to avail the services and facilities offered by FAFLCCs. The services of FAFLCCs are being utilized well by the public, especially by students and parents intending to avail educational loans. The bank arranges financial literacy and education programmes in 12 villages allotted to them with special focus on Government and aided higher secondary schools. These classes are intended to provide basic banking concepts to the school children. They have also conducted workshops at Alappuzha and 60 other centres across Kerala to educate the rural folks on financial services offered by banks and the advantages for those availing the schemes. Base level financial literacy training to Kudumbashree groups has also been conducted.

Credit Counselling Initiatives

Credit counselling is a process in which the consumers are educated about how to avoid incurring debts that cannot be repaid. It normally involves negotiating with creditors to establish a debt management plan for the consumers. In India, due to the recent transformations in the retail banking sector, the need for credit among the ordinary consumers has increased drastically. There has been a rapid growth in the areas of consumer loans, housing loans, credit cards, personal loans etc. This had led to the emergence of credit counselling in the country. In this scenario, a few banks working in the public and private sector have taken initiative in this regard.

The "Abhay" counselling centre in various parts of the state of Maharashtra was started by the Bank of India. The "Disha Trust", another organization initiated by ICICI Bank and "Grameen Para Marshkendras" started by the Bank of Baroda are already in operation. These counselling centres assist people on face to face basis as well as on telephone, email, or through letters. Consumers facing problems related to credit cards, personal loans, housing loans approach these centres to get efficient advice to solve their problems. Major features of such centres is that the services are provided free of cost and the centres are manned by retired bank personnel who are experts in this area. Training and awareness camps are organized by such centres to educate people with need to save as well as to familiarize them with the concept of credit cards, impact of minimum charges etc. (Academic Foundation's Continuing Series, 1998).

Financial Literacy Initiatives in Kerala

Kudumbashree Mission: Launched by the Government of Kerala in 1998 for wiping out absolute poverty from the State through concerted community action under the leadership of local self-governments, Kudumbashree is today one of the largest women empowering projects in the country. The programme covers more than 50 percent of the households in Kerala. Built around three critical components—micro credit, entrepreneurship and empowerment—the Kudumbashree initiative has today succeeded in addressing the basic needs of the less privileged women, thus providing them a more dignified life and a better future. Literal meaning of Kudumbashree is prosperity (shree) of the family (Kudumbam). Kudumbashree programs cover about 37 lakh families organized under 2.02 lakh NHGs through 1,061 CDSs.

All NHGs have bank accounts through which members of NHGs have access to savings and credit services of banks. The NHG is acting as intermediary between banks and ultimate beneficiary. At the NHG level, it is observed that there is lack of knowledge about bank procedures, misconceptions regarding interest rates and lack of awareness about banking ombudsmen etc. Kudumbashree has chalked out a comprehensive financial literacy campaign in order to provide a platform for NHGs to be aware of and benefit from formal banking services.

State Bank of Travancore: The SBT is actively pursuing initiatives to improve financial inclusion and financial literacy. 29 villages in Kerala and 14 villages in Tamil Nadu have been allocated to the bank for financial inclusion. The Bank has set up customer service points and commenced enrolments in 18 villages. The products offered under financial inclusion—"SBT-Sahaya Hastham"—umbrella consists of a savings bank account (zero balance), a recurring deposit account and an overdraft (general credit card) for maximum of ₹ 10,000 for the rural poor.

State Level Bankers Committee (SLBC): SLBC Kerala is in charge of monitoring Financial Literacy and Credit Counselling Centres in the state. SLBC Kerala had opened FLCC in each district under the aegis of respective Lead Bank Scheme as part of its financial literacy initiatives. FLCCs opened by Canara Bank are named "Amulya" and those opened by Federal Bank are named "Fedashwas" and the one by IOB is named as "Sneha". Kerala State has the rare distinction of having 17 FLCCs in all its 14 districts as in the case of RSETIs.

Financial literacy—the ability to process financial information and make informed decisions about personal finance—has received growing attention in the developed world, and recently, in the developing world, as a potentially important determinant of household well-being. One of the most straight forward consequences of limited financial literacy may be limited financial market participation. Households that are not familiar with the workings of a bank, for example, are unlikely to open a bank account, and may instead choose to store cash at home.

In India, a variety of steps have been taken by various agencies in the area for spreading financial literacy. The Reserve Bank of India, public sector as well as private sector commercial banks, NABARD, NGOs, SEWA, Sanchayan Society, Kudumbashree etc. are actively participating in promoting financial literacy. An integrated approach to financial literacy of the marginalized people is yet to evolve in Kerala.

Conclusion and Suggestions

Financial literacy skills enable individuals to navigate the financial world, make informed decisions about their money and minimise their chances of being misled on financial matters. Having financial literacy skills is an essential base for both avoiding and solving financial problems, which in turn, are crucial for living a prosperous, healthy and happy life. Financial problems are often the causes for divorce, suicides, mental illness and a variety of other unhappy experiences. Financial hardship can increase isolation, emotional stress, depression and lower self-esteem, which in turn can generate or exacerbate marital tensions that lead to divorce and even to suicide. Financial literacy is first and foremost about empowering and educating people so that they are knowledgeable about finance in a way that is relevant to their lives and enables them to use this knowledge to make informed decisions.

Financial literacy plays a pivotal role in today's complex financial market. It is an essential component of the empowerment of all categories of people as it gives them an understanding of how to manage finances in a real economy in order to avoid unnecessary hardships, excessive debt and possible financial exclusion. Moreover, it enables people to improve their understanding of the financial opportunities that the formal financial market offers to them. Some of the suggestions for improving financial literacy as follows:

1. Establish an 'Institute for Financial Literacy' with the support of all stakeholders in the area especially financial institutions to impart structured training programmes on financial literacy on a need basis focusing, as discovered through our study, on imparting borrowing literacy-efficient ways of raising funds, availability of avenues, living within means etc.
2. Programs and delivery strategies of the proposed Institute should be oriented towards financial capacity building targeted towards specific groups and should be as personalised as possible.
3. Regulations should be passed to mandate every lending institution (banks, NBFCs, gold loan NBFCs etc.) to educate the marginalised people of every other avenue of funds of equivalent or lower cost.
4. Provide holistic, generic and non-commercial financial education to employees in their place of work through accessible resources and seminars delivered by experienced and specially trained professionals.
5. Arrange 'Finance Behaviour Modification Programmes' for the marginalised people with the support of Kudumbashree and similar projects.
6. Financial literacy programs should start at school, as students and parents need to be educated as early as possible. Government should pay attention to incorporate

into the curriculum, key issues related to money management.

7. Methodologies to assess existing financial literacy programmes should be developed.
8. Financial literacy initiatives should be part of the corporate social responsibility (CSR) and the corporate sector should earmark a percentage of annual profit for the same.
9. Commercial banks should not mix the financial dealings of the marginalised people with that of high profile customers. A separate department with specially oriented personnel should be in charge of dealings with these people who are untapped treasures at the bottom of the pyramid and who were successfully included by corporate business giants in their business journey.
10. The Government of India, the Reserve Bank of India, National Stock Exchange, banks and other private financial institutions should initiate financial literacy programs under the financial inclusion initiative among low income households.
11. Introduction of family workshop sessions on money management that would encourage participants to bring their adolescent children and adult household members. This family session would allow other members of the participants' household to learn about the basic principles of personal financial management and to better understand their role in family finances and how they can contribute to the participants' efforts to budgeting, managing expenses, and savings.
12. With regard to rural sample respondents, they carry debt commitment. Creating awareness among rural population about budget preparation, money management and saving practices can help improve their lives. Proper education at frequent intervals should be conducted about money management relating to how to prepare and follow the budget, how to reduce the expenditure and to save more.
13. Improving basic literacy would be a stepping stone to

improve knowledge on advanced financial literacy.

References

ANZ Bank (2008), "The ANZ Survey of Adult Financial Literacy in Australia", The Social Research Centre, Department of Financial Inclusion and Capability, The Australia and New Zealand Banking Group Limited (ANZ), Australia, available at: http://www.anz.com/Documents/AU/Aboutanz/AN_5654_Adult _Fin_Lit_Report_08_Web_Report_full.

Financial Literacy Foundation, Australia (2008), "Understanding Money", Money Management Portal by Australia, available at: http://wwwunderstandingmoney101.com.

Fox, J., Bartholomae, S. and Lee, J. (2005), "Building the Case for Financial Education", *Journal of Consumer Affairs*, Vol. 39, pp. 195-214.

Gallery, Natalie, Cameron, Newton and Chrisann, Palm (2010), "A Framework for Assessing Financial Literacy and Superannuation Investment Choice Decisions", Paper presented at 18th Annual Colloquium of Superannuation Researchers, University of New South Wales (UNSW), Sydney, Australia, July 12-13.

Hiroshi, Fujiki and Cheng Hsiao (2002), "Public Opinion Survey on Household Financial Assets and Liabilities", Institute for Monetary and Economic Studies, Bank of Japan, IMES Discussion Paper Series, No. 2008-E-17.

HM Treasury, (2007), "Financial Capability: The Government's Long Term Approach".

Holzmann, Robert (2010), "Bringing Financial Literacy and Education to Low and Middle Income Countries: The Need to Review, Adjust and Extend Current Wisdom", World Bank, IZA and CES Revised Draft, July 1, Discussion Paper No. 56501.

Huston, Sandra (2010), "Measuring Financial Literacy", *The Journal of Consumer Affairs*, Vol. 44, p. 296.

Joseph, Job (2012), "Financial Literacy of Economically Marginalised People of Kerala", doctoral thesis, M.G. University.

Lusardi, Annamaria (2008), "Household Saving Behaviour: The Role of Financial Literacy", Information, and Financial Education Programs, NBER Working Paper No. 13824.

Lusardi, Annamaria and Tufano, Peter (2009), "Education, Debt Literacy, Financial Experiences and Over indebtedness", Paper

Presented at the OECD-Brazilian.

MAS (2005), "National Financial Literacy Survey", First National Financial Literacy Survey by Monetary Authority of Singapore July 30.

OECD (2005), "Improving Financial Literacy: Analysis of Issues and Policies", Directorate for Financial and Enterprise Affairs, OECD.

PACFL, USA (2008), President's Advisory Council on Financial Literacy, "Annual Report to the President", available at: http://www.jumpstart.org/assets/files/PACFL_ANNUAL_REPORT_1-16-09.

Prahalad, C.K. (2010), "The Fortune at the Bottom of the Pyramid", revised and updated 5th anniversary edition, Dorling Kindersley India Pvt. Ltd., Noida.

RBI and OECD (2010), "Delivering Financial Literacy: Challenges, Strategies and Instruments", RBI-OECD International Workshop on Financial Literacy, Bengaluru, March 22-23.

Remund, D.L. (2010), "Financial Literacy Explicated: The Case for a Clearer Definition in an Increasingly Complex Economy", *The Journal of Consumer Affairs*, Vol. 44, pp. 276-279.

Reserve Bank of India (2005), "Mid-term Review of Annual Policy Statement 2005-06", Statement by Dr. Y.V Reddy, Governor, Reserve Bank of India.

Reserve Bank of India (2005), "Report of the Internal Group to Examine Issues Relating to Rural Credit and Microfinance", RBI Publications, Mumbai.

Reserve Bank of India (2008), "Financial Inclusion by Extension of Banking Services: Use of Business Facilitators/Business Correspondents", RBI Circular, RBI/2008-2009/455, BC.74/22.01.009/2007-2008, April 24, Reserve Bank of India, Mumbai.

Serrao, Manohar V., Sequeira, A.H. and Hans, V. Basil (2012), "Designing a Methodology to Investigate Accessibility and Impact of Financial Inclusion", in Gangadharan, K. (ed.), 'Financial Inclusion and Inclusive Growth: Scope and Dimension', Reference Press, New Delhi.

Task Force on Financial Literacy (2010), "Canadians and Their Money: Building a Brighter Financial Future", Report on Recommendations on Financial Literacy, prepared by Task Force on Financial Literacy, Canada.

World Bank (2008), "Financial Literacy Survey Questionnaire", Financial Literacy Questionnaire designed by the World Bank, and implemented in Russia in June 2008 in preparation for the Financial Literacy Program.

Worthington, Andrew C. (2006), "Predicting Financial Literacy in Australia", Faculty of Commerce, School of Accounting and Finance, University of Banking Group Limited (ANZ), Australia.

4

Financial Inclusion in Rural India

C. Krishnan

Introduction

We are living in an era of inclusive growth. From the Eleventh Five Year Plan onwards, India has upheld the idea of inclusive growth. This ideal objective can be achieved only when the masses are able to access financial services from formal agencies without any hurdles. Though many efforts in this direction began from the setting up of Co-operative credit Societies in the 1920s, the goal of financial inclusion (FI) is still a dream in our country. Financial inclusion broadens the resource base of the financial system by developing a culture of savings among a large segment of rural population and plays its own role in the process of economic development (Chakrabarty, 2011, 2013; Mundra, 2016).

Further, by bringing low income groups within the perimeter of formal banking sector, financial inclusion protects their financial wealth and other resources in exigent circumstances. Financial inclusion also mitigates the exploitation of vulnerable sections from the usurious money lenders by facilitating easy access to formal credit. FI as a policy initiative entered the banking lexicon only after the recommendations of the Rangarajan Committee in 2008. The Committee defined financial inclusion as the process of ensuring access to financial services and timely and adequate credit where needed by vulnerable groups such as weaker sections and low income groups at an affordable cost (Government of India, 2008).

Financial inclusion, broadly defined, refers to universal access to a wide range of financial services at a reasonable cost. These include not only banking products but also other financial services such as insurance and equity products (The Committee on Financial Sector Reforms, 2009, Chairman: Dr. Raghuram G. Rajan). *Financial inclusion is globally considered as a critical indicator of development and well-being of the society.* FI is considered as an effective means to sustainable economic growth, and is intended to ensure that each citizen of the country is able to use their earnings as a national financial resource for redeployment in productive sectors of the economy (Rao, 2018; Charan Singh, 2014).

Attempts have been made by the policymakers and financial institutions to bring large sections of the rural population within the banking system having realized that financial inclusion is the essence of sustainable economic growth and development in a country like India. Inclusive growth becomes impossible without financial inclusion. Financial inclusion is also a must for the economic development of the country. Without financial inclusion we cannot think of economic development because a large chunk of total population remains outside the growth process. Though our country's economy is growing in a single digit, still the growth is not inclusive with the economic condition of the people in rural areas worsening further.

One of the typical reasons for poverty is being financially excluded, according to several studies (Arunachalam, 2008; Leyshon, 1995; Mohan, R., 2006; Srikanth, R., 2013). Though there are few people who are enjoying all kinds of services from savings to net banking, but still in our country around 40 percent of people lack access to even basic financial services like savings, credit and insurance facilities. India is second only to China in the number of people excluded from financial facilities.

It is in this background that this paper examines the experiments with financial inclusion in India on the part of the Central Bank of the country and the Government of India. The first section of the paper explicates the measures of both the RBI and the Government. In the second section, an attempt is made to discuss the revelations of various committees and agencies on financial inclusion. In the last section, the concluding observations are presented.

Financial Inclusion Initiatives by RBI and Government

The issue of financial exclusion among people, particularly among rural folk, can be addressed only through proper evaluation of the existing supply and demand side constraints. The important supply side constraints in rural areas are: poor banking infrastructure; low resource base of credit purveying institutions; security-based lending procedures; lengthy and cumbersome formalities; low level of financial literacy among people; long distance between customers and bank branches; improper bank operation timings to meet the needs of rural folk; cumbersome documentation and procedures; unsuitable products and language and hostile staff attitude etc. The important demand side constraints are inadequate human capital; skewed distribution of land including lack of proper land reforms; presence of large section of landless labourers; poor state of physical infrastructure; undeveloped social capital; low productivity leading to low level of profitability; poor linkages; poor risk mitigation mechanism; low income; lack of awareness and social exclusion among the rural communities.

Considering the above constraints, financial inclusion has received special emphasis in the growth strategies of India recently. In recent years, development programmes are being implemented with equal or more stress on inclusive aspects particularly financial inclusion in rural areas. The following are some of the important measures/initiatives adopted by the RBI in India to ameliorate financial exclusion in the rural areas.

Initial efforts at financial inclusion were taken up by both the Government and the RBI. Realising the social and economic imperatives of broader financial inclusion, both Government and the Reserve Bank of India have pursued this goal over the last several decades, despite limited success. Ever since the Nationalization of banks, priority sector lending requirements, launching of Lead Bank Scheme, establishment of regional rural banks (RRBs), Service Area Approach, and Self-help Group-Bank Linkage Programme have been some of the leading initiatives. All these innovative programmes were launched with the aim of taking banking services to the masses. Starting in 1990s, however, the focus shifted to strengthening financial institutions as part of financial sector reforms. Despite all the above efforts, the extent of financial exclusion has remained staggering. The Committee on Financial Inclusion headed by Dr. Rangarajan suggested several measures to accelerate the pace of financial inclusion.

The RBI has initiated a number of measures to facilitate financial inclusion. Some of these measures include the following:

- Adoption of a bank-led model for achieving financial inclusion and removing all regulatory bottlenecks in achieving greater financial inclusion in the country.
- Advise to all the banks to open basic saving bank deposit (BSBD) accounts with minimum common facilities such as no minimum balance, deposit and withdrawal of cash at bank branch and ATMs, receipt/credit of money through electronic payment channels, facility of providing ATM card etc.
- Relaxed and simplified KYC norms to facilitate easy opening of bank accounts, especially for small accounts with balances not exceeding ₹ 50,000 and aggregate credits in the accounts not exceeding ₹ 1 lakh a year.
- Simplified branch authorization policy to address the issue of uneven spread of bank branches under which scheduled commercial banks (SCBs) are permitted to freely open branches in Tier 2 and Tier 3 cities with population of less than 1 lakh under general permission, subject to reporting. In North-Eastern Sates and Sikkim, domestic SCBs can open branches without having any permission from the RBI. With the objective of further liberalizing, general permission to domestic SCBs (other than RRBs) for

opening branches in Tier 1 centres, subject to certain conditions.

- Compulsory requirement of opening branches in unbanked villages under which banks are directed to allocate at least 25 percent of the total number of branches to be opened during the year in unbanked (Tier 5 and Tier 6) rural centres.
- For opening of intermediate brick and mortar structure, for effective cash management, documentation, redressal of customer grievances and close supervision of BC operations, banks have been advised to open intermediate structures between the present base branch and BC locations.
- Public and private sector banks have been advised to submit board approved three year Financial Inclusion Plan (FIP) starting from April 2010.
- Banks have been advised that their FIPs should be disaggregated and percolated down up to the branch level.

Pradhan Mantri Jan Dhan Yojana (PMJDY)

Pradhan Mantri Jhan Dhan Yojana (PMJDY), the ambitious and comprehensive financial inclusion scheme was announced by Prime Minister Narendra Modi on August 15, 2014. The objective of Pradhan Mantri Jan Dhan Yojana is to ensure access to various financial services like availability of basic savings bank account, access to need based credit, remittances facility, and insurance and pension to the excluded sections i.e. weaker sections and low income groups. This deep penetration at affordable cost is possible only with effective use of technology.

PMJDY is a National Mission on Financial Inclusion encompassing an integrated approach to bring about comprehensive financial inclusion to all the households in the country. The plan envisages universal access to banking facilities with at least one basic banking account for every household, financial literacy, and access to credit, insurance and pension facility. In addition, the beneficiaries would get RuPay Debit card having inbuilt accident insurance cover of ₹ 1 lakh. The plan also envisages channelling all Government benefits (from Centre/State/Local Body) to the beneficiary accounts and pushing the Direct Benefits Transfer (DBT) scheme of the Union Government. The technological issues like poor connectivity and online transactions would need to be addressed. Mobile transactions through telecom operators and their established centres such as 'cash out points' are also planned to be used for financial inclusion under the scheme. Also, an effort is being made to reach out to the youth of this country to participate in this Mission Mode Programme.

The Government has decided to continue National Mission for Financial Inclusion PMJDY with the following modifications: (a) to continue the National Mission for Financial Inclusion (PMJDY) beyond 14.8.2018, (b) existing over draft (OD) limit of ₹ 5,000 to be raised to ₹ 10,000, (c) there will not be any conditions attached for OD up to ₹ 2,000, (d) age limit for availing OD facility to be revised from 18-60 years to 18-65 years, and (e) under the expanded coverage from "every household to every adult", accidental insurance cover for new RuPay card holders to be raised from ₹ 1 lakh to ₹ 2 lakh under new PMJDY accounts opened after August 28, 2018.

A pipeline has been created for the implementation of PMJDY through which Jan Dhan accounts and mobile banking have been linked to Aadhar (JAM). This pipeline is not only facilitating savings, disbursal of credit, social security, etc., but more importantly is channelizing direct benefits of various government schemes to poor people of the country through the DBT. It has been decided to continue the flagship financial inclusion program (PMJDY) with focus on opening accounts from "every household for every adult". The pipeline of Jandhan-Aadhar-Mobile (JAM) will continue to provide the necessary backbone for coverage of these activities and thereby accelerating the pace of digitalised, financially included and insured society.

An evaluation of the PMJDY shows that the scheme has been clicking up in rural areas. Approximately 32.41 crore Jan Dhan accounts have been opened with more than ₹ 81,200 crore of deposit balance. 53 percent women Jan Dhan account holders and 59 percent Jan Dhan accounts are in rural and semi-urban areas. More than 83 percent operative Jan Dhan accounts (except states of Assam, Meghalaya, J&K) are Aadhaar seeded, with issuance of approximately 24.4 crore RuPay cards to these account holders. More than 7.5 crore Jan Dhan accounts have been receiving DBTs. Banking correspondents (BCs) have been deployed in 1.26 lakh sub-service areas, (rural areas), each catering to 1,000-1,500 households.

Nearly 13.16 crore Aadhar Enabled Payment System (AePS) transactions took place through BCs during the month of July 2018. 13.98 crore subscribers under Pradhan Mantri Suraksha Bima Yojana (PMSBY) with 19,436 claims, involving an amount of ₹ 388.72 crore have been settled so far. Similarly, 5.47 crore subscribers under Pradhan Mantri Jeevan Jyoti Bima Yojana (PMJJBY) with 1.10 lakh claims, involving an amount of ₹ 2,206.28 crore have been settled so far. 1.11 crore persons have subscribed for the Atal Pension Yojana (APY).

Extent of Financial Exclusion in India

The statistics on financial exclusion in India provides a very depressing picture. Out of over 600,000 rural habitations in the country, only about 30,000 or just 5 percent have a commercial bank branch. Just about 40 percent of the population across the country has bank accounts and this ratio is much lower in the North-Eastern part of the country. The proportion of people having any kind of life insurance cover is as low as 10 percent and the proportion having non-life insurance is an abysmally low at 0.6 percent. People having debit cards comprise only 13 percent and those having credit cards, a marginal 2 percent. However staggering these figures may seem, they still convey only part of the extent of financial exclusion in India. Even after 70 years of Independence, around 10 crore households are not connected with the banking sector. Bringing every household within the grasp of the banking system has been an ongoing process that started a decade ago.

There are a number of studies concerning the extent of financial exclusion in India. A few such sources of information are provided here for the benefit of readers.

NSSO 59th Round Survey Results

- 51.4 percent of farmer households are financially excluded from both formal/informal sources.
- Of the total farmer households, only 27 percent have access to formal sources of credit; one-third of this group also borrowed from non-formal sources.
- Overall, 73 percent of farmer households have no access to formal sources of credit.
- Across regions, financial exclusion is more acute in Central, Eastern and North-Eastern regions. All three regions together accounted for 64 percent of all financially excluded farmer households in the country. Overall indebtedness to formal sources of finance of these three regions accounted for only 19.66 percent.

Government of India, Population Census 2011

As per Census 2011, only 58.7 percent of the households were availing banking services in the country. However, as compared with the previous Census of 2001, availing of banking services increased significantly largely on account of increase in banking services in the rural areas.

CRISIL Financial Inclusion Index (Inclusix)

- In June 2013, CRISIL for the first time, published a comprehensive financial inclusion index (viz. Inclusix). For constructing the index, CRISIL identified three critical parameters of basic banking services, namely, branch penetration, deposit penetration and credit penetration.

- The CRISIL Inclusix indicates that there is an overall improvement in financial inclusion in India.
- CRISIL Inclusix (on a scale of 100) increased from 35.4 in March 2009 to 37.6 in March 2010 and to 58.0 in March 2016.

RBI Working Paper Study

Sadhan Kumar (2011) worked out an index on financial inclusion (IFI) based on three variables namely penetration (number of adults having a bank account), availability of banking services (number of bank branches per 1,000 population) and usage (measured as outstanding credit and deposits). The results indicate that Kerala, Maharashtra and Karnataka have achieved high financial inclusion, while Tamil Nadu, Punjab, Andhra Pradesh, Himachal Pradesh, Sikkim, and Haryana have been identified as having medium financial inclusion.

Report of the Committee on Medium-term Path on Financial Inclusion

The Committee on Medium-term Path on Financial Inclusion (CMPFI) was set up in 2015 to devise a measurable and monitorable action plan for financial inclusion that encompasses both households and small businesses. The report highlights that India does not compare very favourably with regard to financial inclusion even with peer emerging market economies. In 2014, over 50 percent of Indian adults held an account with a financial institution, compared to close to 70 percent of adults in various BRICS economies, and an even higher percentage of adults in the US and UK. Similarly, in 2014, 6 percent of Indian adults had borrowed from a formal financial institution in the past 12 months compared with 10 percent or more in other BRICS economies. Furthermore, as of 2014, there were only 18 ATMs per 1,00,000 adult population in India against over 65 in South Africa and over 180 in Russia. Similarly, 10 percent of individuals aged 15 years and above had made payments through debit cards in India as against approximately 40 percent in South Africa.

World Bank's Financial Access Survey Results

The World Bank survey results reveal that in our country, financial exclusion measured in terms of bank branch density, ATM density, bank credit to GDP and bank deposits to GDP is quite low as compared with most of developing countries in the world.

Current Status of Financial Inclusion in the Country

Various initiatives have been taken up by the RBI/Government of India in order to ensure financial inclusion. These include: nationalization of banks, expansion of bank branch network, establishment and expansion of co-operative and regional rural banks (RRBs), introduction of priority sector lending, Lead Bank Scheme, formation of self-help groups (SHGs) and State-specific approach for Government sponsored schemes to be evolved by State Level Banker's Committee (SLBC). During 2005-2006, RBI advised banks to align their policies with the objective of financial inclusion. Further, in order to ensure greater financial inclusion and increasing the outreach of the banking sector, it was decided to use the services of NGOs/SHGs, MFIs and other civil society organizations as intermediaries in providing financial and banking services by the use of Business Facilitator and Business Correspondent Model.

All India Rural Financial Inclusion Survey, 2016-17

NABARD launched a comprehensive survey titled 'NABARD All India Rural Financial Inclusion Survey' (NAFIS) in 2016-17 with a wide coverage. This survey sought to assess the penetration of various aspects of financial inclusion, both in quantitative and qualitative terms. Besides covering economic indicators like savings, debt, income, expenditure and investment, the composition and pattern of consumption, parameters such as borrowing behaviour, financial literacy/knowledge, Kisan Credit Card (KCC), usage of FI technology, distress events (such as crop failure, death of earning member), insurance coverage for crop insurance, life and accident insurance, pension, etc. were included in the survey. The study found that more than half of the agricultural households in the country had outstanding debts, and their average outstanding debt was almost as high as the average annual income of all agricultural households. It was revealed that 52.5 percent of the agricultural households had an outstanding loan on the date of the survey. For non-agricultural households in rural India, the figure was 10 percentage point lower, at only 42.8 percent.

With regard to the sources of borrowing, 43.5 percent of the agricultural households reported to have borrowed money from one source or the other. About 60.4 percent of agricultural households had borrowed from institutional sources alone. About 30.3 percent had borrowed from only informal sources and 9.2 percent of agricultural households borrowed from both the sources. About 56.7 percent of non-agricultural households and 58.6 percent of all households had borrowed from institutional sources. According to the study, only 10.5 percent of agricultural households were found to have a valid Kisan Credit Card at the time of the survey. Households, who had the card, utilized 66 percent of the sanctioned credit limit.

In view of the overarching goal of NAFIS, the overall status of financial literacy was analysed using the data of the survey. The result is provided in Table 4.1.

Overall assessment of respondents on financial literacy indicates that only about 11 percent of the total respondents could fare in the category of having 'good financial literacy'. This indicates that there were about 11 percent respondents who had sound knowledge (score of 3 on financial knowledge score); positive financial attitude (score of 3 or above on financial attitude scale); and having positive financial behaviour (score 6 or above on financial behaviour scale). The figures indicate that individuals living in semi-urban areas and those belonging to non-agricultural households were faring somewhat better compared to their counterparts. However, on the whole, the current status of financial literacy leaves much to be desired in order to reach an acceptable level, making individuals capable of making sound financial decisions for themselves as well as their households.

Table 4.1: Extent of Financial Literacy in India, 2017

Respondent characteristics		Percent of respondents with good financial literacy
All Respondents		11.3
By Location of Households		
	Rural	10.7
	Semi-urban	14.9
By Type of Households		
	Agricultural	10.6
	Non-agricultural	12.1
By Sex of Respondent		
	Male	11.3
	Female	11.2
By Educational Status of Respondent		
	Illiterate	9.4
	Literate without formal schooling	12.5
	Up to primary	11.4
	Class 6th to 10th	11.4
	Senior secondary	13.0
	Diploma/certificate course	9.7
	Graduate	13.6
	Post-graduate and above	16.7

Source: *NAFIS, 2016-17*, NABARD.

Global Findex (GFX)

Besides domestic measurement of FI, there are global institutions such as World Bank that measure the progress of FI across countries. World Bank started capturing data on FI in 2011, once in three years. The latest edition of the Global

Findex (GFX), which came out in 2017, shows that 515 million adults worldwide opened an account at a financial institution or through a mobile money provider between 2014 and 2017. This means that 69 percent of adults globally now have an account, up from 62 percent in 2014, and 51 percent in 2011. In high-income economies, 94 percent of the adults had an account; in developing economies the figure was 63 percent. There is also a wide variation in account ownership across countries.

India's GFX was 35 in 2011, 53 in 2014, and 80 in 2017. This reflects a speedy improvement in FI, suggesting that relevant Indian policies in the last few years have worked well. GFX 2017 stands at 80 for China (79 in 2014), 76 for Russia, 70 for Brazil, 69 for South Africa, 96 for UK, and 93 for US. Given the constraints of poverty, illiteracy, and lack of spread of banking network, the progress under PMJDY is laudable.

Conclusion

Financial inclusion is an accepted objective of the Government ever since the submission of the Report of the Committee on Financial Inclusion. Keeping up the spirit of financial inclusion, the Reserve Bank of India and the Government have initiated several schemes to reduce financial exclusion. On the occasion of the 67th Independence Day of India, our Honourable Prime Minister Sh. Narendra Modi had announced the first ambitious programme of his government titled 'Pradhan Manthri Jan Dhan Yojana (PMJDY)'. He has termed the scheme as National Mission for Financial Inclusion, which carries at the core of development philosophy of '*Sab Ka Sath Sab Ka Vikas*'.

The objective of the scheme is inclusion of all households in formal financial system by opening at least one account of every household in banks, preferably of women members of the household at zero balance. It is a fact that Jan Dhan Yojana marks a landmark in the quest for universal financial access. However, the quality of the PMJDY needs to be taken care of.

Depite these efforts, it is seen from various studies that financial inclusion is still a dream. The latest study commissioned by the NABARD reveals that only 11 percent of respondents in the Survey had 'good financial literacy'. About 30.3 percent borrowed from only informal sources and 9.2 percent of agricultural households borrowed from both the sources.

It is these estimates which tell the reality of financial inclusion. We have to go miles to cover cent percent financial inclusion. This is especially true in rural areas of the country. Financial literacy is a pre-requisite for speedy financial inclusion. The recent report of NABARD reveals the low level of financial literacy in the country. Hence, more concerted efforts are necessary to cover the whole country under the umbrella of financial inclusion.

References

Arunachalam, Ramesh S. (2008), "Scoping Paper on Financial Inclusion: Considerations and Recommendations for UNDP", United Nations Development Programme.

Chakrabarty, K.C. (2011), "Financial Inclusion and Banks: Issues and Perspectives", RBI Bulletin, November.

Chakrabarty, K.C. (2013), "Financial Inclusion in India: Journey So Far and the Way Forward", Keynote address at Finance Inclusion Conclave Organised by CNBC TV 18 at New Delhi.

Chattopadhyay, Sadhan Kumar (2011), "Financial Inclusion in India", RBI Working Paper Series.

Garg, S. and Parul Agarwal (2014), "Financial Inclusion in India: A Review of Initiatives and Achievements", *IOSR Journal of Business and Management*, Volume 16, Issue 6, pp. 52-61.

Government of India (2008), "Report of the Committee on Financial Inclusion in India", Chairman, Dr. C. Rangarajan.

Leeladhar, V. (2005), "Taking Banking Services to the Common Man", Financial Inclusion Speech at the Fedbank Hormis Memorial Foundation at Ernakulum, December 2.

Leyshon, A. and N. Thrift (1995), "Geographies of Financial Exclusion: Financial Abandonment in Britain and the United States", Transactions of the Institute of British Geographers, New Series Publications.

Mohan, Rakesh (2006), "Economic Growth, Financial Deepening

and Financial Inclusion", Address to Annual Banker Conference at Hyderabad, November 3.

Mundra, S.S. (2016), "Financial Inclusion in India: The Journey So Far and the Way Ahead", Deputy Governor, Reserve Bank of India, Speech, BRICS Workshop on Financial Inclusion, Mumbai, September 19.

Raghuram, G. Rajan (2009), "A Hundred Small Steps: Report of the Committee on Financial Sector Reforms".

Reserve Bank of India (2015), "RBI Report of the Committee on Medium-term Path on Financial Inclusion", Chairman: Deepak Mohanty.

Reserve Bank of India (2009), "Financial Inclusion: An Overview", Occasional Paper, Mumbai.

Singh, Charan (2014), "Financial Inclusion in India: Select Issues", working paper no. 474, Indian Institute of Management, Bangalore.

Srikanth, R. (2013), "A Study on Financial Inclusion: Role of Indian Banks in Reaching Out to the Unbanked and Backward Areas", *International Journal of Applied Research and Studies*, Volume 2, Issue 9, September.

Thorat, Usha (2007), "Financial Inclusion: The Indian Experience", Financial Inclusion Conference, White Hall Palace, London, UK, July.

5

Interest Free Micro Finance as an Alternative to Financial Inclusion

Muhammed Palath

Introduction

Poverty is a global problem which exists in all countries, developed as well as developing. Poverty is a pronounced deprivation in well-being and comprises of many dimensions. It includes low income and the inability to acquire basic goods and services necessary for survival with dignity. From 2005, the World Bank has raised the measure of global poverty line to US$ 1.25 per day. The number of people who lived in absolute poverty, i.e. below US$ 1.25 a day was 1.29 billion in 2008, equivalent to 22 percent of the population in the developing world. Though poverty has declined in the developing countries and the world as a whole, its progress has been uneven region-wise, and in terms of sheer number and magnitude it still remains a bewildering problem in several developing countries like India. According to the World Bank [1] estimate, 32.7 percent of the population of India is below the poverty line in terms of US$ 1.25 per day. This comes to a whopping figure of 35 crore, accounting for one-third of the absolute poor in the world.

During the post-Second World War period, developing countries like India adopted several strategies for poverty eradication depending upon the dominant paradigm of the age. During the 1960s and 1970s, purely growth oriented strategies were experimented pinning faith on trickle down hypothesis. On realising that trickledown effect failed to work, India initiated programmes aimed at directly attacking poverty which consisted of directly providing the poor with adequate purchasing power through employment generation and asset creation and access to food grains through food subsidy programmes. Though the poverty ratio declined during 1980s and 1990s, the programmes in fact failed in delivering the goods, as it resulted in underutilisation of resources and mismanagement largely due to corruption, bureaucracy and political interference. [2]

In the wake of disenchantment with direct approach to poverty eradication, there has been realisation on the part of the development economists that the major reason why the poor are unable to participate in the development process is financial exclusion. There exists a near consensus among development economists now, that financial inclusion is a necessary condition for poverty eradication as it will improve the capability of the poor. Financial inclusion is the ease of access, availability and usage of the formal financial system by all members of the economy. These include not only banking products but also other financial services such as insurance and equity products. The major reasons for non-accessibility of finance to the poor, among others, include lack of collaterals, absence of trust, and high cost of credit.

The failure of commercial banking to provide financial services to the poor coupled with the disadvantages of using informal markets are major reasons for intervention in the market for financial services at the micro level. Consequently, micro finance emerged as a development approach aimed at addressing the financial needs of the deprived sections of the society. The term micro finance refers to "the provision of financial services to low income clients, including self-employed, low income enterprises in both urban and rural areas" (Ledgerwood, 1999). [3] The chief factors which characterised micro finance system that developed in the initial (successful) phase were: (a) financial services at door step, (b) absence of collateral, (c) low rate of interest, (d) high rate of repayment and (e) development of entrepreneurial skills. These factors granted a popular interest in micro finance, and developing countries as well global development organisations like World Bank and United Nations took keen interest in popularising this as an effective mechanism for poverty eradication in the Third World nations.

After the turn of the 1990s, the micro finance sector in many countries attracted investors, both foreign and indigenous, to build and fund these institutions as they became a safe haven for investment. The reason was that the poor people were good borrowers, return on capital was very high, and repayment of loan was nearly 100 percent. The double edged benefits not only attracted private equity firms into micro finance sector but also enabled them to raise money by floating shares even at a high premium. Thus, MFIs began to be moulded to cater to the requirements of wealthier class. The shareholders were naturally expecting huge profits for their investment. The pressure started mounting on the companies and typical target sales and profit maximisation tactics slowly crawled into the nerves of once benevolent institution which ultimately resulted in the defeat of the laudable objectives of micro finance movement itself. Several studies carried out in different parts of the world have drawn pointed attention to the evils that crept into the programme overtime.

Micro finance which was hailed as an effective tool for poverty eradication and economic empowerment of the poor, of late, has fallen into disrepute for several reasons. Most important among them is high rate of interest charged by micro finance institutions. Recent studies carried out even in countries known for the success of micro finance such as Bangladesh and Latin America revealed that MFIs charged interest rates varying from 20 percent to 40 percent. This is higher than even the usurious rates charged by village money lenders. (Surya, 2005, [4] Khandker, Shahidur R., 1998) [5] The resultant debt trap coupled with forced recovery methods perpetrated on the borrowers led to a large number of farmer suicides in countries like India which in turn cast a dark shadow on micro finance. (Sharma, Surinder) [6]

A general allegation levelled against the programme is that

it has failed to reach the poorest of the poor. A comprehensive study of 13 micro credit schemes in Asia, Africa, and South America showed that the benefits of micro credit schemes were not scale neutral, the upper and middle income poor benefiting more than the poorest of the poor. (Hume, D., 2000) [7] This happened because micro financiers considered lending to the bottom poor as extremely risky as compared to the top poor. Even in the limited areas in which micro finance was successful in eradicating poverty, it was due to the availability of subsidised funds these institutions were able to receive from funding agencies. (Khandker, Shahidur R., Khalily, Baqui and Khan, Zahed, 1995) [8] Conventional micro finance institutions have also been criticised for their failure to create entrepreneurial skills among the poor, for the funds provided to them were not used for productive purposes but for subsistence expenditures on food, houses etc. (Wright and Graham, 2000) [9]

Interest Free Micro Finance

Interest free micro finance is basically rooted on the principle of interest free banking developed by a team of Muslim economists in the 1970s with a view to getting rid of the evils of interest (*riba*) which has been strictly prohibited by Islam. Interest free banking is based upon two principles. Firstly, money according to Islam is a medium of exchange and a store of value and not a commodity as viewed by the conventional economists and therefore cannot be lent out against interest. Secondly, interest is in itself an unjust institution as it ensures a guaranteed return to the lender of money while the borrower (entrepreneur) is exposed to all the risks. Instead of interest, Islam promotes profit and loss sharing. Hence, interest free banks are also known as Islamic banks. Inculcating ethics or values with financial transaction is the hallmark of Islamic financial institutions.

The main feature which distinguishes Islamic micro finance from its conventional counterpart is the concept of social responsibility and working for the common good. Eradication of poverty, socio-economic justice and equitable distribution of income are among the primary goals of Islam and the salient features of an Islamic economic system. The philosophical basis of the Islamic financial system is that of *al-adl* (social justice) and *al-ihsan* (benevolence) which should be reflected in its operations. In other words, the spirit of the entire Islamic economics and financial system is based on the concept of 'social justice' by ensuring equitable distribution of wealth and income among members of the society.

There are mainly two models of interest free micro finance, profit-based and charity-based. Charity-based institutions are functioning with the sole objective of poverty eradication. These institutions mainly depend on zero return finance. The important feature of these institutions is the implementation of various educational and livelihood programmes to make poorest of the poor economically active and lift them above the poverty line. Profit-based institutions are using both zero return finance and participatory finance. Participatory finance is used for development of micro enterprises and other productive activities. Most of these institutions have become sustainable by meeting their operational expenses from their profits. Charity-based institutions are meeting their expenses from donations, charities and from grants. For mobilising the working capital, both types of institutions depend on different sources including savings, shares, donations, grants, *zakah* (compulsory charity), *waqf* (endowments) etc.

Different Business Models of Interest Free Micro Finance

Considering the method of operation of each micro finance institution, they are classified into different models. There are lots of interest free institutions working at the international level, practicing different models. The peculiarity of interest free micro finance institution is that it has diverse models to apply for various types and needs of the clients. For satisfying different types of members in micro finance institutions, various institutions have been practicing different business models simultaneously.

***Mudaraba* Model (Trustee Partnership):** This model is applied for micro enterprise development. Suppose, a small entrepreneur wants to start a business unit, but he has no money as capital. Then, he approaches an interest free micro finance institution. The institutions conduct a study about the feasibility of his project and trust worthiness of the client. If all reports are positive, the institution allows enough funds as capital. Here, micro finance unit and the micro enterprise act as partners, the MFI investing money and the micro entrepreneur investing in labour. If profit is positive, sharing according to the proportions specified in the agreement is allowed. When the profit is negative, the financial loss is borne by the MFI. In this case, the loss to the micro entrepreneur is his labour and efforts.

***Murabaha* Model (Cost-Plus Sale):** Under this model, a micro finance unit makes available durable consumption goods like vehicles, machineries etc. to the clients on deferred payment basis. When a customer approaches the MFI for financing a particular good, the institution buys goods and resells them to micro enterprises. Here, the MFI is fixing the price with the cost plus as a mark up for covering the administrative costs. The borrower often pays for the goods in equal instalments or pays in lump sum within a specified period of time.

***Musharaka* Model (Joint Venture):** In *musharaka*, micro entrepreneurs and Islamic micro finance institutions jointly invest in the productive\ undertaking. Suppose an auto driver wants to purchase an auto for his employment and he has half of the total investible amount. The auto driver the approaches the MFI and after the feasibility study, MFI invests the other half. The reward and responsibilities are fixed in advance. The representative of the MFI assures proper management of the micro enterprise by timely auditing of its accounts. The profit is shared according to the pre-determined proportion and the loss is shared according to the capital contribution.

Micro Finance with *bai'salam* (Deferred Delivery Sale)

This model is commonly used by MFIs working among the farmers. Here, micro entrepreneurs such as small farmers and producers sell their product in advance to the interest free micro finance institution and receive the entire price. Goods are transferred within the time period mentioned in the contract. As we know farmers need money in the beginning stage of the cultivation, in interest-based system, these needs are met by raising loans at huge rates from money lenders and MFIs. In case of a crop failure/loss, the farmers face indebtedness and enter into a debt trap. Very low price during the harvesting season is another problem. Here, in the *bai'salam* model, the MFI determines the price and purchases the product in advance with full payment. The commodity is then transferred within the time period specified.

Ijara Model of Micro Finance

Ijara means leasing. Leasing is a product used by MFIs to raise income for the institution. Producers, farmers and households need different types of equipments and machineries. But they do not have the capacity to purchase the same. Micro finance institutions buy equipments and machines for productive activities and lend it out to the clients. Here, the clients pay rent to the institutions.

Al wadiah (Safe-keeping)

Micro finance units aim at providing different types of financial services including micro saving. Promotion of savings habit among the poor is essential for poverty alleviation. Therefore, MFIs use different types of savings programmes. Most of the micro finance institutions are receiving deposits in the form of thrifts. Like conventional institutions, there are no interest payments on savings. But the amount is kept safely and returned when the client demands it or after the completion of a specified period of time.

***Wakala* Model (Agency Contract):** Micro finance institutions act as an agent to provide loans to their members on a priority basis. The working capital is mobilised through donations, *zakah* funds and thrift collection of members. Few institutions also receive grants from international donor agencies and from the government. The MFIs thus act as an agent of donor agencies or government to eradicate poverty by extending loans and other micro finance activities.

Qard hasana Model (Benevolent Loan)

In this system, a micro finance institution works only for giving micro credit. Funds are transferred without receiving any return to meet urgent needs of the client. The capital is mobilized by using donations, *zakah* funds and other grants. For meeting the working expenses, a service charge is collected from the borrowers.

Ar-rahn Model (Pledging)

When people needs money for urgent transaction purposes, one of the ways to seek it is from financial institutions by pledging gold. Conventional financial institutions are charging high rate of interest for the same. But lots of interest free financial institutions are working in different countries on interest free basis and they are serving the same function.

Ar-rahn means simply gold loan. Micro finance institutions are lending money by receiving gold as collateral. A service charge is levied on the beneficiaries for meeting the operational expenses.

It is against this background that interest free micro finance (Islamic microfinance) has been suggested as a viable alternative to the conventional interest based micro finance. The present paper attempts to examine the role of Islamic micro finance in alleviating poverty.

Objectives of the Study

The overall objective of the present study is to examine the role of interest free financing institutions in alleviating poverty in Kerala .The specific objectives of the study are as under:

- To examine the socio-economic and religious backgrounds of the beneficiaries of micro finance in the study area.
- To discuss the modus operandi of Islamic micro finance institutions.
- To capture the impact of micro finance on beneficiaries in terms of increase in income, employment and reduction in poverty.
- To identify major problems faced by interest free micro finance institutions in the study area.

Hypotheses

- Islamic micro finance acts as a tool for financial inclusion and poverty alleviation.

Growth of Islamic Micro Finance Institutions in Kerala

Kerala accounts for the largest number of MFIs functioning in India. As per the latest available statistics, the total number of institutions in Kerala comes to almost 500. Bulk of them is registered under the Charitable Society's Act and charitable trusts as non-profit enterprises. The rest are registered as finance companies. There is an umbrella organisation, INFACC, to coordinate, guide and supervise these institutions. As per official records, presently there are 390 institutions registered with INFACC.

Like the rest of India, MFIs in Kerala also began to come up after the turn of 1970s. Between 1970 and 1995, the number of institutions increased from 6 to 59. Since then, there has been very rapid growth, reaching 390 in 2010. Thereafter, the growth rate began to slow down. District-wise distribution of IMFIs in Kerala is shown in Table 5.1. The largest number is in Malappuram, the only Muslim majority district in the state, Kozhikode Ernakulum, Thrissur Palakkad and Kannur districts follow in the same order.

Table 5.1: Number of Interest Free MFIs in Kerala under INFACC

District	Interest free units
Kasargod	5
Kannur	27
Kozhikode	72
Wayanad	3
Malappuram	165
Palakkad	27
Thrissur	28
Ernakulum	32
Kottayam	1
Alappuzha	4
Idukki	0
Pathanamthitta	0
Kollam	12
Thiruvananthapuram	14
Total	390

Methodology of the Study

The study is largely based upon primary investigation carried out among 30 interest free micro finance institutions, randomly chosen in proportion to the district strength from 390 units registered with INFACC. From each of the 30 units, 10 beneficiaries were selected applying the lottery method. Secondary data was drawn from different sources including magazines, newspapers, published reports etc.

For the analysis of data, both quantitative and qualitative techniques were made use of. Important quantitative techniques used included arithmetic mean, correlation, regression, chi-square test and t-test.

Operation of Interest Free Institutions

Mobilization of Funds: The functioning of MFI can be explained in terms of methods usually adopted by interest free banking institutions for mobilisation and deployment of funds.

Interest free banks raise funds through: (a) current account deposits, (b) savings account deposits, and (c) investment account deposits. In the case of the first two accounts, no return is offered as these deposits are usually made for the convenience of customers and safe custody. In Islamic terminology, these deposits are known as *alwadia* or *amana* deposits.

These deposits can be withdrawn by the depositors without notice. Investment accounts are meant for profitable investment projects and are operated on *mudaraba* principle. According to this principle, the depositors are treated as financiers of capital and the bank as an entrepreneur and the returns are shared between the depositors and the bank on the basis of profit-loss sharing principle.

Islamic micro finance institutions in Kerala by and large follow the mobilisation methods cited above but with certain differences. Seed capital for these institutions is generally raised through the shares of founder members motivated by social welfare considerations, rather than profit motive.

Once the institution comes into being, further mobilisation of funds for working capital purposes is effected through: (a) pigmy savings of the beneficiaries, (b) voluntary contributions of individuals in the form of *zakah*, *sadaqa* and *waqaf*, and (c) the public's share in the institutions, mainly with a view to promoting this noble venture.

In the case of sample units, 72 percent of the total capital consisted of shares, 22 percent savings and voluntary contributions at 6 percent (Table 5.2). One important point that can be inferred from the table is that shares and savings accounted for 94 percent of the total capital, which in fact indicates the saving potential of these institutions.

The savings potential of 30 sample units works out to ₹ 9.22 crore, i.e. an average of ₹ 30.73 lakh per unit. Applying this average to the total number of institutions in the state, would give roughly ₹ 120 crore as the gross saving potential of the MFIs in Kerala.

Table 5.2: Details of Sources of Working Capital

Type of source	Number of units	Amount of capital (₹ lakh)	Percentage (amount)
Shares from members	12	704.52	71.96
Deposits/pigmy savings	24	217.40	22.20
Own capital	24	33.59	3.43
Grants	4	18.76	1.91
Loans	1	4.81	0.49
Total	65	979.08	100.00

Deployment of Funds: The Islamic micro finance institutions working in Kerala do not follow all the methods mentioned above, as most of these methods are generally adopted by institutions working with commercial motives. Since institutions in Kerala are floated with the major consideration of helping the poor and the destitute, the dominant method followed is that of *qardhasan.* However, there are a few institutions which use participatory financing methods of *mudaraba* and *musharaka*.

Table 5.3 shows that all the 30 sample units provided *qardhasan* loans and the total amount came to ₹ 7.04 crore during the year 2010-11. Only 12 institutions utilised funds for participatory financing which amounted to ₹ 6.35 crore. The profit earned from this dealing amounted to ₹ 86 lakh (14 percent). This means that profit earned from these ventures is greater than the current market rate of interest, which indicates that opportunities for profitable investment are not rare in Islamic micro finance sector.

Collateral Security: In sanctioning loans, conventional banks and financial institutions insist upon physical collaterals. Conventional micro finance institutions generally do not demand physical collaterals, but insist on mutual guarantee of members. Interest free MFIs in Kerala practice both. In the sample, half of them demanded physical collateral of gold, land deeds, or other assets, and the remaining half insisted on personal guarantee or mutual guarantee as in the case of SHGs.

The lone NBFC working in Kerala insisted on physical guarantee of land deeds. Needless to say, the presence of physical collateral is a hurdle in financial accessibility by the poor. By providing loans without collaterals, interest free institutions ensure financial accessibility to the poor.

Table 5.3: Details of Advances on Participatory Basis, 2010-11

	Mudaraba	*Musharaka*	Direct investment	Total	*Qard hasana*
Number of institutions	8	3	1	12	30
Amount utilised (in lakhs)	84.2	547.39	3.0	634.59	703.6
Profit earned (in lakhs)	3.70	82.76	na	86.46	Nil

Service Charge: In order to cover the working expenditure, the IMFIs charge a nominal fee known as service charge which varies from ₹ 2 to ₹ 50 per loan among the sample units. There is no uniform pattern in this respect, as some of them charge a fixed amount per loan regardless of the amount of loan, while in some other cases service charges vary with the amount of the loan. However, there are few units which do not take any service charge.

Duration of Loan: Banks and other financial institutions these days focus on long-term loans while micro finance institutions give importance to short-term loans (Table 5.4). This method of MFIs is followed by Islamic MFIs in Kerala also as is clear from the table. More than two-thirds of the loans are very short-term (less than six months), remaining one-third relates to medium-term (less than three years) and short-term (less than one year). Not a single unit was found giving long-term loans.

Purpose of Loans: The purpose for which finance is provided is influenced, to a great extent, by the aims of the financing institutions. The major aim of MFIs in Kerala as mentioned earlier is amelioration of poverty or the empowerment of the poor. Table 5.5 portrays that 19 percent of the loans were given for the purposes of employment creation and income generation (agriculture, business, self-employment, micro enterprise), 28 percent for human resource development (medical treatment, education), 16 percent for basic needs (housing, drinking water, sanitation), 20 percent for consumption purposes (living expenses and durable consumption goods), and 16 percent for old loan repayment. Needless to say, most of the purposes mentioned above are basic needs, both from the perspective of Islam as well as mainstream economics.

Table 5.4: Duration of Loans

Duration	Percentage of total loans
Very short-term, less than 6 months	67.68
Short-term, less than a year	23.55
Medium-term, up to 3 years	8.77
Long-term, up to 5 years	0
Very long-term, more than 5 years	0
Total	100

Table 5.5: Zero Return Loans during 2010-11

Purpose of loan	Number of loans	Percentage
Self-employment/employment	661	7.37
Business/agricultural inputs	1,045	11.65
House/sanitation/drinking water	1,433	15.97
Treatment	1,347	15.00
Education	1,192	13.28
Consumption/Living expenses	1,746	19.46
Old loan repayment	1,409	15.70
Others	137	3.45
Total	8,970	100.00

Defaults: Most studies show that the repayment rate of micro finance institutions is well above that of banking institutions in the organised sector. Repayment rate as reported by our sample units was even higher than the conventional MFIs. Of the 30 sample units, 15 had reported defaults. However, the default rate reported accounted for only a negligibly small percentage (0.3 percent) of the amount lent. Under these circumstances, it may be noted, that in conventional micro finance, forced methods are often adopted for recovery. Such methods are conspicuous by their absence in the Islamic system. In the Islamic MFIs, in the event of repayment failure, the term of repayment is extended by the institutions or they resort to moral suasion. In general, in this system, default is not a serious problem.

Mode of Repayment: Micro finance institutions which concentrated on short-term loans collected the loan amount on regular intervals—daily, weekly, bi-weekly, monthly and quarterly basis. While sanctioning loans, they usually seek the option of repayment from the customers. In the sample, no unit reported daily repayment. Nine units insisted upon weekly repayment. Bi-weekly and monthly repayment systems were followed respectively by 8 and 7 units. In 6 units, no such direction was found.

Impact of Interest Free Micro Finance in Kerala

Having examined the operational aspects of the micro finance institutions, we shall now turn to examine their impact on those who availed finance from these institutions.

The total number of persons who borrowed funds from 30 samples units stood at 16,148. The district-wise distribution of beneficiaries as well as units is shown in Table 5.6. The largest number of units and beneficiaries was in Malappuram district followed by Kozhikode and Palakkad. The average number of beneficiaries per unit was the highest in Palakkad followed by Ernakulam and Thiruvananthapuram.

Socio-economic and Religious Profile of the Beneficiaries: In a study focusing on poverty eradication, it is necessary to examine the socio-economic characteristics of the beneficiaries with a view to identifying the poor. The socio-economic variables considered for the purpose were income, assets, savings, employment, education, gender, age, religion, and marital status.

Table 5.6: District-wise Distribution of Beneficiaries

District	Number of members	Number of institutions	Percent of members	Percent of units	Average members
Kasargod	100	1	0.62	3.33	100
Kannur	430	2	2.66	6.67	215
Kozhikkode	2,258	6	13.98	20	376
Malappuram	8,357	13	51.75	43.33	642
Palakkad	1,927	2	11.93	6.67	963
Thrissur	390	2	2.41	6.67	195
Ernakulam	1,686	2	10.44	6.67	843
Kollam	200	1	1.24	3.33	200
Trivandrum	800	1	4.95	3.33	800
Total	16,148	30	100	100	538

Economic Status: The most important factor affecting poverty is the economic status of the households. Income and assets are the two variables which determine the economic status.

Family income as reported by the beneficiaries is portrayed in Table 5.7. As there is generally a tendency on the part of individual respondents to under report income, we have attempted to minimize the errors involved by cross-checking. Only 3 percent of beneficiaries came from families having a monthly income above ₹ 10,000 (US$ 185).

Table 5.7: Family Income of Beneficiaries

Income status	Numbers of clients	Percent of total
Up to ₹ 4,000	108	36
₹ 4,001-8,000	160	53.33
₹ 8,001-10,000	22	7.33
₹ 10,001 and above	10	3.33
Total	300	100

Planning Commission of India had fixed the poverty line in rural areas as ₹ 26 per day per person in 2011. A five member family accordingly will need almost ₹ 3,900 to become non-poor. Applying this norm, 36 percent of the population would fall below the poverty line. If we consider the international poverty line of US$ 1.25 per day, 97 percent of the beneficiaries will fall below the poverty line. This finding points to the fact that Islamic micro finance institutions serve the poorest of the poor. This finding assumes importance in view of the fact that conventional micro finance institutions generally cater to the rich poor.

Asset Position: The picture about the asset position of beneficiaries is given in Table 5.8.

Table 5.8: Economic Status of Clients

Type of assets	Numbers of beneficiaries	Percentage
Land	261	87.00
House	254	84.67
Livestock	23	7.67
Business	50	16.67
Lab/equipments	7	2.33
Shop	20	6.67
Durable consumption goods	127	42.33
Jewellery	108	36.00
Vehicles	58	19.33
Others	1	0.33

Source: Primary Data.

Land Ownership: Land is considered as the most important asset. Ownership of land is presented in Table 5.9. Thirteen percent of the beneficiaries had no land at all. A little less than half of the total beneficiaries had less than 5 cents of land. One of the norms stipulated by the Government of Kerala for choosing beneficiaries of poverty eradication programmes implemented in the state is that the concerned person should not have more than 5 cents of land. If we consider this norm, 61 percent of the beneficiaries will fall below the poverty line.

Table 5.9: Land Ownership by Beneficiaries

Area of land	Numbers of beneficiaries	Percentage
No land	39	13.00
Below 5 cents	145	48.33
5 to 10 cents	77	25.67
10 to 20 cents	24	8.00
20 cents and above	15	5.00
Total	300	100.00

Occupational Status: The occupational status of beneficiaries is shown in Table 5.10. Number of aggregate people employed comes to 179, constituting 64 percent. Bulk of them was self-employed and wage employed. Those employed in the government sector constituted only 5 percent. 110 of the beneficiaries were housewives, of whom many were prepared to go for outdoor employment to make up for low family income, provided job opportunities are available. However, we did not include housewives among the employed, following the usual procedure. Unemployment rate stood at 3.6 percent only.

Table 5.10: Types of Employment of Beneficiaries

Employment type	Numbers of beneficiaries	Percentage
Self employed	66	22.00
Wage employed	76	25.33
Government job	15	5.00
Private job	22	7.33
No job	11	3.67
Housewife	110	36.67
Total	300	100.00

Educational Status: A cursory glance at Table 5.11 throws light on the low educational status of a vast majority of beneficiaries. 82 percent of the beneficiaries had attained education level below SSLC. Those having a degree and above qualification accounted for a negligible 5 percent. This points to the low social status of the beneficiaries in general.

Table 5.11: Educational Status of Beneficiaries

Educational status	Numbers of beneficiaries	Percentage of total
Illiterate	5	1.67
Lower primary	62	20.67
Upper primary	62	20.67
High school and SSLC	119	39.67
Higher secondary/diploma	37	12.33
Degree	11	3.67
Above degree	4	1.33
Total	300	100

Religious Status: Of the total respondents, Muslims accounted for the largest number at 237 (79 percent). The remaining 21 percent were from the Hindu community. This shows the fact that even though these institutions are exclusively organised and managed by Muslims, its benefits are open to all communities, irrespective of the religious affiliation. In fact, in sanctioning loans, these institutions take into consideration the trustworthiness of the borrowers and the size and urgency of their needs. This is also in conformity with the Islamic tradition. In the classical periods of Islam, there were several cases in which even *zakah* proceeds were distributed to the non-Muslims citizens.

Vast majority of beneficiaries belonged to economically, socially and educationally backward sections. Among the beneficiaries, a sizable number were non-Muslims. Thus, the MFIs in Kerala are designed to meet the needs of the poorest of the poor, irrespective of religious and caste considerations.

Impact Analysis of Islamic Micro Finance in Kerala

Though Islamic micro finance is essentially a poverty eradication programme, it provides funds for various purposes, some of which need not directly contribute to income generation or employment creation. But such apparently non-productive purposes as conduct of marriage or repayment of old loan, may indirectly contribute to poverty reduction, as in their absence individuals may be compelled to dispose of some of their assets or to avail interest ridden loans, which may worsen their vulnerability. Therefore, in order to evaluate the impact of MFIs on the beneficiaries we have followed a two-level approach.

- To evaluate the impact in terms of the extent of fulfilment of the purpose for which a loan is taken by a customer.
- In terms of the extent of income generation, asset creation and employment creation resulting from the utilization of borrowed funds.

The first one was evaluated by ascertaining from the clients the purposes for which funds were borrowed, and whether the purpose was fulfilled fully, partly or not at all. Various purposes for which funds were borrowed are given in Table 5.12.

Table 5.12: Distribution of Beneficiaries According to Purpose of Loan Taken

Purpose of loan	Number
Living expenses/durable consumption	79
Working capital/Agri. inputs	54
Education	18
Employment	24
Medical treatment	26
House construction/repair	49
Repayment of old loan	32
Vehicle	2
Micro enterprise	4
Marriage	12
Total	300

In Table 5.13, the distribution of beneficiaries according to the level of fulfilment/non-fulfilment is given. Nearly three-fourths of the beneficiaries reported that their purposes were fully attained. Only in three percent of the cases, non-fulfilment was reported.

Table 5.13: Fulfilment Level of Purpose

	Numbers of clients	Percentage of total
Fully fulfilled	220	73.33
Partially fulfilled	70	23.33
Not fulfilled	10	3.33
Total	300	100.00

The various types of purposes can be classified into: (a) creating employment, (b) increasing income, (c) reducing debt burden, (d) escaping from debt trap, and (e) reducing vulnerability. The cases of 290 fully or partially fulfilled beneficiaries relating to the five broad classes of purposes is shown in Table 5.14. It created employment for 63 persons, increased income of 75, reduced debt burden of 168, reduced vulnerability of 162 and salvaged 156 from the debt trap. Thus, Islamic micro finance appears to have produced a very positive impact on the economy by way of economic empowerment and vulnerability reduction.

Table 5.14: Fulfilment of Clients' Purposes

Purpose	Numbers of clients	Percentage of total
Create employment	67	22.33
Increase income	73	24.33
Reduce debt burden	168	56.00
Escape from interest trap	156	52.00
Reduce vulnerability	162	54.00

We also tried to find out the reasons for the non-fulfilment. The most important reasons reported by the beneficiaries were small amounts of loans sanctioned and very short duration of repayments insisted. People may require large amounts for purposes like house construction and medical treatment. Most of these institutions can meet only a small fraction of such requirements. Though the clients need long-term loans for certain purposes, these institutions issue loans only for short periods not exceeding one year.

Increase in Income: It has been already noted that income of 73 persons out of 300 increased. Since increase in income is a reflection of poverty reduction, we shall further probe into the details of increase in income. Table 5.15 shows the distribution of beneficiaries according to the magnitude of income increase, as reported by them. The table shows that while the income of one-third of population increased less than ₹ 2,000 per month, the income of one-fifth increased between ₹ 4,000 and ₹ 8000. Income of another 8 percent increased more than ₹ 10,000 per month, indeed a very substantial increase. The persons whose income increased by more than ₹ 10,000, borrowed money to seek jobs in the Gulf countries.

Table 5.15: Average Increase in Monthly Income

Increase in income (₹)	Number of beneficiaries (percent)	Cumulative numbers (percent)
Up to 2,000	33	33
2,001-4,000	18	51
4,001-6,000	8	59
6,001-8,000	2	61
8,001-10,000	4	65
10,000 and above	8	73
Total	73	

It may be worthwhile to know which occupational categories recorded increase in income. The occupational categories considered were wage employed, self-employed, private job, government job and no job. As is clear from Table 5.16, all occupational categories reported an increase in income. P-value of the t-test shows that income increase was more significant in the case of self-employed. It was least significant in the case of government jobs. Interestingly, income increase was significant in the case of no job category as well. This is because in our sample, housewives came under the no job category. Some housewives had taken loans from these institutions for purchasing simple production equipments like tailoring machines with a view to making small earnings.

Table 5.16: Mean Difference in Income in Pre-loan and Post-loan Periods

Occupation categories	Period	N	Mean income (₹)	SD of income (₹)	T stat	p-value one tail
Wage employed	Pre-loan	76	5368.421	2232.14	2.497	0.007
	Post-loan		5934.210	3496.04		
Self-employed	Pre-loan	63	6253.968	5046.46	4.361	0.000
	Post-loan		9165.079	7077.27		
Private job	Pre-loan	22	5340.909	1984.38	3.530	0.001
	Post-loan		6454.545	1851.05		
Government job	Pre-loan	15	5400.000	1594.63	2.085	0.028
	Post-loan		6466.666	2669.05		
No job	Pre-loan	124	5643.548	2761.79	3.057	0.001
	Post-loan		5780.645	2751.16		
Total	Pre-loan	300	5665.670	3189.162	5.668	0.000
	Post-loan		6614.000	4349.664		

We have already identified the asset background of beneficiaries in terms of land ownership. It may be pertinent to examine the association between land ownership and increase in income. Table 5.17 shows that the association is significant in the case of two categories, those having less than 5 cents and those having greater than 20 cents (as indicated by p-values). A plausible explanation is that the landless mainly borrow funds for meeting living expenses and hardly anything for productive purposes. Those who own more than 20 cents belonged to the middle class who often borrow for purposes of purchasing consumer durables and house repair.

Table 5.17: Mean Difference in Income in Pre-loan and Post-loan Periods and Ownership of Land

Area of land owned	Period	N	Mean income (₹)	SD of income (₹)	t-stat	p-value one tail
No land	Pre-loan	38	5955.26	3265.77	1.327	0.112
	Post-loan		6928.94	5668.54		
Below 5 cents	Pre-loan	146	5777.39	3801.10	4.861	0.000
	Post-loan		6941.09	4801.04		
5 to 10 cents	Pre-loan	77	5720.77	2348.70	2.630	0.005
	Post-loan		6298.70	3459.60		
10 to 20 cents	Pre-loan	24	5083.33	1691.84	2.967	0.003
	Post-loan		5937.50	1843.39		
20 cents and above	Pre-loan	15	4533.33	1552.26	1.381	0.094
	Post-loan		5333.33	2319.69		

We have also looked into the association between educational status and the increase in income. In the case of illiterates, the association is not at all significant. Those having SSLC qualification show the highest significance, followed by primary and higher secondary. Degree and above depicted a very low significance. Probable reason for this relationship is that the bulk of the illiterates belong to vulnerable sections who borrow money largely for living expenses. In the case of degree holders and above, they were mainly interested in white collar jobs and normally borrowed for house construction/repair purpose, purchase of vehicles, conduct of marriage etc. (Table 5.18).

Impacts on Employment Generation: Employment creation helps poverty amelioration through income increase. Employment creation may occur either on part-time or full-time basis. Here, a person is considered in full-time employment provided he is able to depend fully on any single job obtained with the assistance from micro finance, for earning his livelihood. If one is constrained to depend on any other job than the one acquired with the help of micro finance, he is considered to be on part-time employment. Of the 67 borrowers employed, 15 were on full-time and 36 on part-time basis. Self-employed were separately treated for their peculiar nature (Table 5.19).

Table 5.18: Mean Difference in Income in Pre-loan and Post-loan Periods and Educational Status of Beneficiaries

Educational status	Period	N	Mean income (₹)	SD of income (₹)	t-stat	p-value one tail
Illiterate	Pre-loan	5	7300.00	248.99	nil	nil
	Post-loan		7300.00	248.99		
Lower primary	Pre-loan	62	4846.77	1567.05	3.066	0.002
	Post-loan		5419.35	1893.03		
Upper primary	Pre-loan	62	5693.54	3126.24	2.437	0.008
	Post-loan		6379.03	4424.86		
High school/ SSLC	Pre-loan	119	5743.69	3363.48	4.438	0.000
	Post-loan		6978.15	4520.39		
Higher secondary/diploma	Pre-loan	37	6494.59	4739.43	2.911	0.003
	Post-loan		6954.05	4717.02		
Degree and above	Pre-loan	15	5766.66	1801.45	1.382	0.094
	Post-loan		8566.66	7724.88		

Table 5.19: Employment Created by Interest Free Loan

Type of employment	Numbers of beneficiaries	Percentage
Full-time employment	15	5.00
Part-time employment	36	12.00
Self-employment	16	5.33
Total	67	22.33

Financial Inclusion: It is almost an accepted fact among development economists that financial exclusion is a major cause of perpetuation of poverty. An attempt has been made in our enquiry to identify the extent of financial inclusion effected by micro financing. For this purpose, we sought information from the beneficiaries regarding their savings with and loans taken from other financial institutions. Of the 300 beneficiaries, 157 availed loans from interest based banks,

NBFIs and money lenders. The remaining 143 persons did not avail loans from any institutions other than IMFI. Coming to savings, 141 persons reported that they had savings only with Islamic micro financing institutions. This indicates that nearly half of the beneficiaries who were formerly excluded had now been brought within the ambit of financial inclusion as a result of the operation of Islamic micro finance institutions.

As hinted earlier, half of the beneficiaries were compelled to approach other interest ridden institutions largely due to the inability of Islamic finance institutions to provide large funds, and long-term finance. In fact, this is a major limitation of the Islamic micro finance institutions operating in Kerala.

Problems of Interest Free Institutions

We have attempted to elicit from the informants, institutions and beneficiaries, the problems confronted by them. The institutions were operating under several constraints. The most important constraint for the operation of these institutions related to the guidelines of the Reserve Bank of India which regulates and controls the functioning of the financial institutions in the country. One major problem of these institutions is with respect to mobilization of funds. As per the existing rules of the RBI, deposit mobilization from the public is permitted for banks and NBFCs against interest only. Deposit mobilization on the basis of post facto determined return like profit is disallowed. Since the interest free institution offers only profit, these institutions cannot be registered as banks. Moreover, the CRR and SLR requirements insisted by RBI is another hurdle in the way of deposit mobilization.

Again as per RBI regulations, banks are not allowed to make investments in business activities other than interest based transactions. All the institutions in our sample reported that the regulatory conditions of the RBI were a major obstacle in the smooth and successful operation of interest free institutions. This largely affected their capacity to mobilize sufficient funds. 25 percent of the institutions reported that lack of funds is one important problem.

A sizable number of the beneficiaries reported that since the amount of finance is small and available for very short period of time, the bulk needs of the beneficiaries cannot be fulfilled without assistance from other financial agencies. Few of the beneficiaries complained that some of the IMFIs insist upon security which most of them cannot afford. In general, the regulatory conditions of the banking sector is a major constraint in mobilizing funds as a result of which these interest free institutions are not able to sanction bulk finance. Lack of professionalism is another important problem faced by most interest free institutions in Kerala.

Conclusion

Micro finance as a measure of poverty eradication through financial inclusion emerged in the wake of the failure of poverty eradication methods experimented during 1950s and 1960s. Though micro finance was successful in its initial years, recent studies have shown that it has failed in delivering the goods. The major villain for its failure is interest (*riba*) which has been strictly prohibited by Islam, and not the basic model of micro finance. The basic model, if integrated with Islamic ethical principles such as zero interest, economic and social justice and commitment to social welfare, can go a long way in empowering the poor and ameliorating poverty even in Muslim minority countries where interest based financial system is deeply rooted. This is the lesson one can learn from the experience of Kerala where Islamic micro financing institutions have been working for long. If the concerned governments can promote interest free micro finance institutions by favourably amending the existing banking laws, the poor and down trodden, irrespective of cast and creed will benefit immensely.

Endnotes

1. The World Bank (2011), "Poverty in India", cite note, World Bank.
2. Roy, Bunker (1996), "Grassroots Struggle in Rajasthan for an End to Corruption", *One World*, May 12.

3. Ledgerwood, J. (1999), "Microfinance Handbook: An Institutional and Financial Perspective", Washington D.C.: The World Bank, pp. 1-2, 63-90.
4. Surya (2005), "On Microfinance", Women's Newstoday, September 21.
5. Khandker, Shahidur R. (1998), "Fighting Poverty with Micro Credit: Experience in Bangladesh", New York: Oxford University Press Inc.
6. Thilo Kunzemann (2008), "Can Micro-credits Fight Poverty or are they a *Debt Trap* for the Poor?", January 16, Allianz Knowledge Partner site.
7. Hulme, D. (2000), "Is Micro Credit Good for Poor People? A Note on the Dark Side of Microfinance", Small Enterprise Development, Vol. 11, No.1, pp. 26-28.
8. Khandker, Shahidur R., Khalily, Baqui and Khan, Zahed (1995), "Grameen Bank Performance and Sustainability", World Bank Discussion Papers, No. 306, The World Bank, Washington D.C.
9. Wright, Graham (2000), "Microfinance Systems: Designing Quality Financial Services for the Poor", New York: Zed Books Ltd.

6

Level of Financial Literacy and Inclusion

Sini VT

Introduction

Financial inclusion means delivery of banking services at an affordable cost to different sections of the disadvantaged and low income groups. Access to finance by the poor and vulnerable groups is a perquisite for poverty reduction and social cohesion. In fact providing access to finance is a form of empowerment of the vulnerable groups. The various financial services include credit, savings, insurance and payments and remittance facilities. The objective of financial inclusion is to extend the scope of activities of the organized financial system to include within its ambit people with low incomes.

Through graduated credit, the attempt must be to lift the poor from one level to another, so that they can come out of poverty. Financial inclusion is a state in which all people have access to appropriate, desired financial products and services in order to manage their money effectively. It is achieved by financial literacy and financial capability on the part of the consumer and financial access on the part of product, services and advice suppliers. The effort of all institutions—both financial and development—is aimed at encouraging inclusion. The use and access of financial services has been at the stem of study for major regulatory financial institutions. Some developed countries report annually on the level of access of finance for economic and social developments. Technology is gaining grounds in banking services through the use of ICT devices. Some of the various ways of encouraging and ensuring financial inclusion includes circulation of deposit accounts, loans, insurance and automated electronic transfers.

Financial Inclusion in India

Post-Independence, the major focus of the Government and the Reserve Bank of India was to develop a sound banking system that could support planned economic development through mobilization of resources and channel them to productive sectors. Accordingly, the Government and the RBI used the banking system as an important agent of change. The RBI setup a commission (Khan Commission) in 2004 to look into financial inclusion and the recommendations of the Commission were incorporated into the Mid-term Review of the Policy (2005-06). In the Report, RBI insisted on the banking sector with a view of achieving greater financial inclusion to make available a basic "no-frills" banking account.

In India, financial inclusion first featured in 2005, when it was introduced, that, too as a pilot project in the Union Territory of Puducherry, by Dr. K.C. Chakraborthy, the chairman of Indian Bank. Mangalam Village became the first village in India where all households were provided banking facilities. In addition to this, KYC (know your customer) norms were relaxed for people intending to open accounts with annual deposits of less than ₹ 50,000. General credit cards (GCCs) were issued to the poor and the disadvantaged with a view to help them access easy credit. In January 2006, the Reserve Bank permitted commercial banks to make use of the services of non-governmental organizations (NGOs/SHGs), micro finance institutions and other civil society organizations as intermediaries for providing financial and banking services.

The Indian banking system will have to deliver on the plan for financial inclusion, the system, which demonstrated its resilience in the face of the global financial crisis, by adopting strong and urgent measures to reach the unbanked segment of the society and unlock their savings and investment potentials. An inclusive financial system has several merits. It facilitates efficient allocation of productive resources and, thus can potentially reduce the cost of capital. Initiatives for financial inclusion have come from the financial regulators, the governments, and the banking industry (Table 6.1).

Table 6.1: History of Financial Inclusion in India

1793	Formal distribution of Taccavi loans
1883	Land Improvement Loans Act to finance agricultural loans to farmers to improve production
1904	Cooperative Credit Societies Act
1928	Subsequent to the Royal Commission on Agricultural in India, Land Mortgage Banks were created
1935	Reserve Bank of India (RBI) set up its Agriculture Credit Department.
1949	RBI was nationalized
1955	Imperial Bank was nationalized and renamed the State Bank of India
1963	Agriculture Refinance Development Corporation was set up
1969	Nationalization of 14 scheduled commercial banks
1970	Lead Bank Committee (F.K.F. Nariman) was formed
1972-76	Setting up of the Rural Electrification Corporation (REC), Small Farmer Development Agency (SFDA) and regional rural banks (RRBs)
1981	Nationalization of 6 scheduled commercial banks
1982	Creation of Nationalization Bank for Agriculture and Rural Development (NABARD)
1989	Service Area Approach (SAA) initiated
1992	NABARD's Self-help Group (SHG)-Bank Linkage Programme
1996	Local Area Banks set up
1997	Targeted Public Distribution System (TPDS) introduced
2005	Task Force on the Revival of Short Term Co-operative Credit Structure (STCCS)
2006	Policy initiative for business correspondents (BCs)/business facilitators (BFs)

contd...

2007	Committee on Financial Inclusion (C. Rangarajan)
2008	Agriculture Debt Waiver and Debt Relief Scheme
2009	The Mahatma Gandhi National Rural Employment Guarantee Act (MGNREGA) came into existence (NREGA since 2005)
2009	Formation of the Unique Identification Number—Aadhaar
2013	Direct Benefit Transfer (DBT) Scheme
2014	PMVVY (Pradhan Mantri Vaya Vandana Yojana)
2014	Credit Enhancement Guarantee Scheme for Scheduled Castes
2014	PAHAL (Benefit Transfer of LPG)
2014	Venture Capital Fund for Scheduled Castes
2015	Pradhan Mandri Mudra Yojana (Micro Units Developmental Refinance Agency)
2015	Conversion of Kisan Credit Card (KCC) to RuPay KCC
2015	From Jan Dhan to Jan Suraksha
2016	Stand Up India Scheme
2016	Digital Financial Inclusion in India
2017	PMJDY (Pradhan Mantri Jan DhanYojana)
2017	Atal Pension Yojana (APY)
2017	PMSBY(Pradhan Mantri Suraksha BimaYojana)
2017	PMJJBY (Pradhan Mantri Jeevan Jyoti BimaYojana)

Financial Literacy

A number of definitions of financial literacy exist in the literature. Basically, 'financial literacy' refers to the knowledge and understanding of financial concepts thereby resulting in the ability to make informed, confident and effective decisions regarding money. Financial literacy can be interpreted broadly or narrowly. In a broader perspective, financial literacy can be stated as "understanding of economics and how economic conditions and circumstances affect household decisions" (Worthington, 2006). A narrow definition of financial literacy focuses on "basic money management tools such as budgeting, saving, investing and insurance" (Natalie, Newton and Chrisann, 2010).

It is the narrow view of financial literacy that is particularly relevant to individual decisions concerning financial matters.

Different interpretations of financial literacy have been used in financial literacy studies resulting in no uniform definition. A number of studies have used financial literacy interchangeably with other names like financial capability, financial empowerment, debt literacy, financial knowledge, and economic literacy. Definitions used by major studies focus on knowledge and ability to make informed judgments to reach an intended outcome such as lifetime financial security and the skills required to realise those outcomes. At the very outset, it is necessary to distinguish between the general and specific meaning of the term financial literacy. The terms 'financial' and 'literacy', both of which are used to represent a myriad of issues can easily lose their relevance when used.

According to Collins Dictionary and Thesaurus, the word 'finance' relates to the words 'economic', 'business', 'commercial', 'monetary', 'fiscal' and 'pecuniary', each of which has its own meaning. 'Literacy', according to the same dictionary, basically means or is synonymous with the ability to read and write; education, learning and knowledge. When these words are combined to form a single term, 'financial literacy', a whole new dimension emerges, which encompasses more than the individual terms listed. Widdowson and Hailwood (2007) in their article 'Financial literacy and its Role in Promoting a Sound Financial System', stated that "for some, financial literacy is a wide-ranging concept, incorporating an understanding of economics and how household decisions are affected by economic conditions and circumstances while for others, it means focusing quite narrowly on basic money management skills—budgets, savings, investment, insurance".

But what does financial literacy mean to the marginalized people who are at the bottom of the economic pyramid in developing countries. Is financial literacy a relevant concern to them? This study is an attempt to prove theoretically and empirically that financial literacy is much more relevant in the case of marginalized people and can be improved through financial education. Financial literacy is a broad concept that includes both financial information and financial behaviour and it is relevant for all people regardless of their wealth or income.

Objectives of the Study

- To study the extent to which tribes of Kerala are financially included;
- To study the extent of financial literacy brought in by financial inclusion efforts among tribes;
- To assess the level of financial literacy among tribes; and
- To examine the accessibility level of financial services such as savings, credit and insurance.

Scope and Significance of the Study

Financial inclusion mainly focuses on the poor who do not have formal financial institutional support and getting them out of the clutches of local money lenders. As a first step towards this, some of our banks have now come forward with general purpose credit cards and artisan credit cards which offer collateral-free small loans.

The study is important because wide range of efforts were put to add socially backward people within the ambit of financial service networks such as banking, micro finance etc. Financial inclusion will help in financial literacy and thereby empowerment of weaker communities which is very vital for nation's development.

Methodology and Database

Method of the Study: The study was descriptive in nature which is based on both primary as well as secondary data.

Source of Data: The data required for the study were collected both from primary and secondary source.

Source of Primary Data: The main source of data for this study was the primary source. Tribal people are the informants of the study. The primary data was collected from the tribal people of the three taluks of the Wayanad district viz. Mananthavady, Sulthan Bathery and Vythiri. The selected 150 respondents included people belonging to various tribal communities such as Paniyas, Kurichyas and Adiyas. For collecting the data from the respondents, a structured interview schedule was used.

Sources of Secondary Data

The secondary data required for the study was collected from:

- Journals
- Periodicals
- Newspapers
- Research dissertations
- Official records

Limitations of the Study

Though the study is comprehensive, it has got its on limitations. It is evident that such limitations are inherent and unavoidable in these types of studies. Efforts have been made to ensure that the research and design is conducted to optimize the ability to achieve the desired objectives. However, there are some constraints that do not validate the research but need to be acknowledged. Major limitations were as under:

- Villages do not have adequate literacy level to respond correctly to the questions intended by the investigator.
- There is possibility of error in secondary data collected from different sources.

Tribes in Wayanad and Financial Inclusion

Kerala holds a unique position in the tribal map of India. According to the 2011 Census, the scheduled tribe population in Kerala stood at 484,839 constituting 1.45 percent of the total population. Every district in Kerala has some tribal population. They are found significantly in the districts of Wayanad, Kannur, Kozhikode, Palakkad and Idukki. These districts encompass around 80 percent of the tribal population in Kerala. However, the main tribal communities are in the taluks of North Wayanad, South Wayanad, Mannarghat, Devikulam and Thodupuzha. As per Census 2011, the highest number of scheduled tribes was recorded in Wayanad (151,443) and the lowest in Alappuzha (6,574).

Wayanad is primarily a rural district, in which 96.2 percent of the total population lives in villages. None of the talukas have a sizable urban population. However, it is to be noted that in the context of Kerala, there is no perceptible difference between rural and urban areas in terms of demography or facilities, as there has always been historical rural-urban continuum with respect to demography, economy and development. Kalpetta (district headquarters), Sulthan Bathery and Mananthawady are the three major business towns of the district. Due to its proximity to Mysore and Kozhikode, along with the fact that the highway passes through the district, people from Wayanad are found moving to both these cities for business and commerce, and also for other employment opportunities.

Wayanad district of Kerala is located in the southern tip of Deccan Plateau lying close to the Western Ghats. It is a quiet place where scenic beauty, wildlife and tradition matters. This land has a history and mystery, culture and social epistemology yet to be discovered. It is located at a distance of about 76 kilometres from the sea shores of Calicut in the Western Ghats. This hill station is full of plantations, forest and wildlife. Wayanad has a history of bloody wars between Vedar Kings and Kottayam Rajas. The war between Pazhassy Raja (Kerala Varma) of Kottayam and Tipu Sultan of Mysore came to an end with the death of Pazhassy Raja in 1805.

The name Wayanad is believed to have been derived from the word Vayal-Nadu—The land of paddy fields. It is the least populated district of Kerala but holds the largest number of tribal population. Wayanad is famous for its rich tribal heritage. Approximately, about four lakh tribes live in Kerala state but half of this population is from Wayanad only. It is believed that these tribes were the original inhabitants of this area. Tribal communities (Adivasis) and non-tribal communities are the two main groups in Wayanad.

The tribal population in the district is found in remote and inaccessible areas. They work as casual labour in agriculture, plantation work and forestry for survival, since they have little or no land. The absence of land holdings, education and health facilities is acute amongst the tribal community. The native Adivasis mainly consist of various sects of Paniyas, Kurichiyas, Adiyas, Kurumas, Ooralis, Kattunaikkas etc. The Kurichyar is the most developed amongst them. They are small land owners, whereas the members of other tribes are mostly labourers. Tribal people have their own unique lifestyle, culture, customs, traditions and religious practices. Tribals do not have a written script. Their history can be traced only through their oral traditions and religious practices. As a result of the changes taking place, even their practices are becoming extinct. Now-a-days many tribals blindly follow the modern culture. As a result, they are losing their unique culture, land, language, etc. They have become a minority community exploited by the others.

Financial inclusion has been one of the top priorities of the Reserve Bank of India during the recent years. The banking industry has shown tremendous growth in volume and complexity during the last few decades. Despite making significant improvements in all the areas relating to financial viability, profitability and competitiveness there are concerns that banks have not been able to include vast segment of the population, especially the underprivileged sections of the society into the fold of banking services. Financial inclusion can truly lift the financial condition and life standards of the poor and the disadvantaged.

The present study aims to find solutions for the following questions.

- Would financial inclusion help in uplifting the ST community in the Wayanad district?
- Would it improve their financial literacy level?
- Are financial services easily accessible to the people?

Profile of Selected Tribal Communities

In the present study, only three major tribal communities in Wayanad district such as Paniyas, Kurichyas and Adiyas have been taken into consideration. A brief profile of these selected tribal communities is given in the following paragraphs.

Paniyas: Paniya tribes are a major tribal community of Wayanad. The word Paniya means worker in regional language Malayalam. Among the tribal people, Paniya tribe have worked as bonded labourers for the landlords in ancient period. The main occupation of these tribes is to work in the field of land owners. They worked as slaves in the ancient period. Most of the people of this community were engaged with agricultural works but some of them were also engaged in tea plantations and coffee estates and construction works. Paniya tribes live together in colonies. Paniya tribes of Wayanad district speak Paniyan language. It is a combination of Malayalam and Kannada but some of the words are independent.

Kurichyas: Kurichyas of Wayanad have a great martial tradition. They were experts in archery. They constituted the army of Kerala Varma Pazhassi Raja, the King of Kottayam, who fought against the British East India Company in several battles. The descendents of those warriors are still expert archers. They were the first migrants into the plateau and started farming. Kurichyas raise several cash crops including pepper. The Kurichya tribes claim themselves superior to all other Hindu tribes. They choose their life partners from their tribe only.

Adiyas: The Adiya tribe is also one of the slave tribe communities in Wayanad. These tribes are known as 'Ravulayar' traditionally. The word Adiya means slave in local language Malayalam. Gadhika is a kind of traditional dance performed by them. The head of the community is called Commikaran.

Tribes and Access to Finance

As finance, in a narrow sense money, has become omnipresent in every part of the country, tribes, a community which still preserves certain reminiscences of their values and cultural system inherited historically, are inclined not to embrace the modernity to a desirable level. Of course, their alienation from the mainstream community is partly attributed to their cultural settings and the value system which they imbibed from their social structures.

In fact, the identity of tribes is entangled with this uniqueness. Having said this, it is apparent that it is practically precarious for tribes to live in isolation from the mainstream at least in respect of using money as a medium of exchange. As they use money for effecting transactions, they must have also come in contact with the banks. Although there may be variations in the extent to which tribes have got connected with the banks by way of possessing bank accounts, it is obvious that in Kerala, a state where banking network has reached every nook and corner, nearly cent percent tribes have got access to bank accounts.

A study into the financial exclusion of tribes in Wayanad district, a tribe concentrated district in the State, has revealed that near 94.8 percent of tribes are having bank accounts (Table 6.2). Within the tribal communities, Kuruma, a forward non-primitive tribe community in the State, has near 98 percent of households with bank accounts (Kumar, 2013). The figure is slightly dismal in the case of Paniya tribe, a backward non-primitive tribe commonly seen in southern India.

Table 6.2: Households with Bank Account

(percent)

Status with bank accounts	Tribal communities			Total
	Kurichias	Paniya	Adiya	
Households with bank account	96.20	93.10	96.60	94.80
Households with no bank accounts	3.80	6.90	3.40	5.20

Table 6.2 gives us a hint that majority of tribal households have come under the sphere of the banking network, and therefore financial inclusion, the first step towards attaining

inclusive economic growth, can be said to have materialized. The picture would be clear if we go further to examine the reason as to why tribes have had a bank account (Table 6.3). Most of the tribes have accessed bank accounts because of a reason which does not have much to with their income and asset status. It is obvious that tribes working under MGNREGA have been mandatorily forced to avail of bank accounts. This means that labour market intervention through the government programmes has provided the necessary impetus in making tribes included in the banking fold.

Table 6.3: Why did Tribal Households Take Bank Accounts

Reasons for bank accounts	Tribal communities			Total
	Kurichias	Paniya	Adiya	
Self decision	11.5	8.4	9.2	29.1
Campaign by banks	5.0	2.3	3.2	10.5
Advice from relatives and friends	1.6	3.1	1.3	5.9
MGNREGA	20.1	14.2	20.2	54.5

Banking institutions, especially in the repercussion of the banking sector reforms, are more curious in expanding their customer base for which naturally they would be interested in offering bank accounts to more people. Further, offering bank accounts to 'unbanked' does not necessitate any effort from the banks both in terms of expense or expertise. Moreover, in the case of MGNREGA and other subsidy programmes by the government, it is an opportunity for the banks to transact government's money through the coffer of the banks. The volume of transaction of banks gets inflated when the funds of government in the name of disbursement of subsidy and other welfare measures are channelized through the banks for credit to the accounts of beneficiaries.

Table 6.4 shows the income-wise classification of the respondents. It can be observed from the table that 86.67 percent of the total respondents had a monthly income of below ₹ 5,000. 12 percent of them had a monthly income between ₹ 5,000-₹ 10,000 and 1.33 percent of them had a monthly income above ₹ 10,000. 68 percent of Adiya people, 100 percent of Paniya people and 92 percent of Kurichya people had a monthly income below ₹ 5,000. 28 percent of Adiya people and 8 percent of Kurichya people had a monthly income between ₹ 5,000-₹ 10,000. 4 percent of Adiya people had a monthly income above ₹ 10,000.

Table 6.4: Income-wise Classification of Respondents

Monthly income (₹)	Adiya		Paniya		Kurichya		Total	
	No.	%	No.	%	No.	%	No.	%
Below-5000	34	68	50	100	46	92	130	86.67
5000-10000	14	28	0	0	4	8	18	12
Above 10000	2	4	0	0	0	0	2	1.33
Total	50	100	50	100	50	100	150	100

The level of financial literacy among the tribal people is analysed in terms of their awareness with regards to various financial terms. Their degree of awareness is measured on a three point scale including high awareness, average awareness and low awareness. The result of the analysis is presented in Table 6.5. It can be observed from the table that no respondent had high awareness with regards to various financial terms. The respondents had average awareness about various financial terms such as bank deposits, bank loans, ATMs and cheque book. They had low awareness about the remaining terms also. Their awareness level was higher with regards to the term 'bank deposits' and awareness level was lower regards the term 'stock market'.

Level of Financial Inclusion

In the present study, the level of financial inclusion was calculated on the basis of the usage of financial services by the respondents. If they were using any of the financial services such as banking, insurance, mutual funds, SHGs, pension funds, post office deposits and non-banking financial services, they were treated as financially included and if they are not using any of the mentioned financial services, they were treated as financially excluded. It can be noticed from the table that 93.33 percent of the total respondents were financially included and the remaining 6.67 percent of them were financially excluded.

Table 6.5: Level of Financial Literacy

Various financial terms	Adiya		Paniya	
	Mean	SD	Mean	SD
Bank deposits	2.32	0.5047	1.3000	0.5440
Bank loans	2.24	0.5014	1.3000	0.5440
ATMs	1.84	0.8889	1.1700	0.4819
Credit cards	1.26	0.6312	1.0200	0.4352
Cheque	1.54	0.8889	1.1700	0.4819
Insurance	1.64	0.8514	1.1700	0.4819
Shares and debentures	1.20	0.4949	1.0000	0.0000
Mutual funds	1.12	0.4352	1.0000	0.0000
Pension schemes	1.60	0.7559	1.1000	0.3031
SHG	1.56	0.5771	1.1600	0.3703
Stock market	1.12	0.4352	1.0000	0.0000
Consumer rights	1.28	0.5361	1.0000	0.0000
Overall	1.56	0.6251	1.1158	0.3035

contd...

Various financial terms	Kurichya		Total	
	Mean	SD	Mean	SD
Bank deposits	2.6400	0.5481	2.0867	0.5323
Bank loans	2.5400	0.5997	2.0267	0.5484
ATMs	2.1800	0.9267	1.7300	0.7658
Credit cards	1.3100	0.6773	1.1967	0.5812
Cheque	2.2400	0.7602	1.6500	0.7103
Insurance	2.0200	0.8204	1.6100	0.7179
Shares and debentures	1.3600	0.6627	1.1867	0.3859
Mutual funds	1.4400	0.7886	1.4267	0.4073
Pension schemes	1.5800	0.8401	1.4533	0.6330
SHG	1.6400	0.8172	1.1267	0.5882
Stock market	1.2600	0.4431	1.1900	0.2928
Consumer rights	1.2900	0.7365	1.1900	0.4242
Overall	1.7917	0.7182	1.4892	0.5489

Source: Primary Data.

When looking at the community-wise analysis, it can be inferred that all respondents of the Kurichya community were financially included. The level of financial inclusion was 96 percent among the Adiya community and 84 percent among the Paniya community. Hence, the level of financial inclusion was higher among the Kurichya people and lower among the Paniya people (Table 6.6).

Table 6.6: Level of Financial Inclusion

Level of financial inclusion	Adiya		Paniya		Kurichya		Total	
	No.	%	No.	%	No.	%	No.	%
Financially included	48	96	42	84	50	100	140	93.33
Financially excluded	2	4	8	16	0	0	10	6.67
Total	50	100	50	100	50	100	150	100

Source: Primary Data.

Level of Usage of Various Financial Services

Table 6.7 shows the level of usage of various financial services by the respondents. It can be noticed from the table that 92 percent of the total respondents were using banking facilities, 40.67 percent were associated with self-help groups, 29.33 percent of them had insurance coverage, 34.67 percent of them were using non-banking financial services, 20.67 percent of them had a post office savings account, 6.67 percent of them were associated with some of the pension funds and 2.67 percent of them were associated with financial markets. None of the respondents were using the mutual fund schemes. 96 percent of Adiya people, 80 percent of Paniya people and 100 percent of Kurichya people were using banking facilities. 48 percent of Adiya people, 8 percent of Paniya people and 32 percent of Kurichya people had an insurance coverage. 84 percent of Adiya people, 30 percent of Paniya people and 8 percent of Kurichya people were associated with self-help groups.

20 percent of Adiya people were associated with one of the pension funds and 8 percent of them were associated with financial markets. However, no respondents from the Paniya and

Kurichya community had access to pension schemes and financial markets. 32 percent of Adiya people, 6 percent of Paniya people and 24 percent of Kurichya people had post office deposits. 32 percent of Adiya people, 32 percent of Paniya people and 40 percent of Kurichya people were using non-banking financial services.

Table 6.7: Usage of Various Financial Services

Various financial services	Adiya		Paniya		Kurichya		Total	
	No.	%	No.	%	No.	%	No.	%
Bank	48	96	40	80	50	100	138	9
Insurance	24	48	4	8	16	32	44	29
Mutual Funds	0	0	0	0	0	0	0	0
SHG	42	84	15	30	8	16	61	40
Pension fund	10	20	0	0	0	0	10	6.6
Financial markets	4	8	0	0	0	0	4	2.6
Post Office Deposits	16	32	3	6	24	24	31	20.6
Non-banking financial service	16	32	16	32	40	40	52	34.6

Source: Primary Data.

Comparison between Various Financial Services

It is important to know the ability of the tribal people to compare one financial service with other services for choosing the right service suitable to them. So, the respondents who were using various financial services were asked to mention whether they had made comparison between various financial services at the time of selecting these services. The result of this analysis is presented in Table 6.8. It can be noticed from the table that 54.29 percent of the total respondents who were using various financial services did not compare one financial service with other services for choosing the right service which is suitable to them. But 31.43 percent of them compared one financial service with the other services.

Community-wise analysis shows that all respondents belonging to the Paniya community, 95.83 percent of Adiya people and 16 percent of Kurichya people did not compare one financial service with the other services. However, 84 percent of Kurichya people and 4.17 percent of Adiya people compared one financial service with other services for choosing the right service suitable to them.

Table 6.8: Comparison between Various Financial Services

Comparison	Adiya		Paniya		Kurichya		Total	
	No.	%	No.	%	No.	%	No.	%
Compared	2	4.1	0	0	42	84	44	31.43
Not compared	46	95.8	42	100	8	16	76	54.29
Total	48	100	42	100	50	100	140	100

Source: Primary Data.

As far as the Kurichya people were concerned, the main reason for opening a bank account was 'for making deposits and availing loans' as it got the highest mean score of 2.36 and S.D. of 0.7494. The second important reason was 'for receiving the remuneration of MGNREGA programme' with a mean of 2.3 and S.D. of 0.8631. The least important reasons were 'for getting any subsidies from the Government' and 'for receiving scholarships' with a same mean score of 1.7 and S.D. of 1.1473 (Table 6.9).

Table 6.9: Reasons for Opening a Bank Account

Sources of influence	Adiya		Paniya	
	Mean	SD	Mean	SD
For receiving the remuneration of MGNREGA Programme	3.48	0.994	2.54	1.541
For making deposits and availing loans	1.92	0.695	1.5	1.129
For getting any subsidies from the government	1.72	0.926	1.66	1.255
For receiving scholarships	1.72	0.926.	1.66	1.255

contd...

Sources of influence	Kurichya		Total	
	Mean	SD	Mean	SD
For receiving the remuneration of MGNREGA Programme	2.3	0.863	2.94	1.177
For making deposits and availing loans	2.36	0.749	2.77	1.269
For getting any subsidies from the government	1.7	1.147	1.93	0.941
For receiving scholarships	17	1.147	1.69	1.110

Source: Primary Data.

Conclusion

Financial literacy is considered as an important factor that promotes financial inclusion. Due to the importance of financial literacy, Reserve Bank of India and Central Government has undertaken many projects and programmes to make people financially literate. Even then many of the individuals are unfamiliar with even the most basic economic concepts needed to make sensible saving and investment decisions. This has serious implications for savings, retirement planning and other financial decisions. In this scenario, a study that covers these issues will be significant. Therefore, the present study focuses on the extent of financial inclusion and the level of financial literacy among a socially excluded group, that is, the tribal people of Wayanad district in Kerala. Wayanad distinct is selected because it is a tribal area and it stands first in the case of adivasi population when compared to other districts of Kerala.

Financial literacy is considered as an important adjunct for promoting financial inclusion and ultimately financial stability. Because of this reason, government authorities are giving much attention to financial literacy programmes. But the problem is that these programmes are not making any impact among a large segment of the population which is socially and economically backward. The present study reveals that the tribal people are poorly informed about various financial products and practices. This is troubling because financial illiteracy may stunt their ability to save and invest for retirement, undermining their well-being in old age.

The real inclusion of disadvantaged people like tribes into the economic system becomes a reality only if formal banking institutions start meeting the credit requirements of these people which definitely would result in mitigating the menace of excess dependence on informal players. It is good to know that some government schemes like MGNREGA programme, micro credit facility etc. have influenced the tribal people to a large extent and have been instrumental in enticing them to open bank accounts. It shows that if a scheme is properly introduced, it will definitely make some desired results. Hence, government agencies have to re-design the financial literacy programmes in such a manner so as to reach the rural masses in large numbers.

Suggestions

- Government agencies and NGOs may undertake financial awareness programmes among the tribal people to increase their financial literacy. This will be helpful in ushering in a practice of recording of income and expenditure among them.
- Banks, insurance companies and other financial service providers may concentrate more on the tribal people because they are not yet fully financially included. It will help the agencies to increase their customer base.
- Authorities may take necessary steps to include financial literacy programmes in the school curriculum. It will help to mould a financially educated new generation.
- While undertaking any tribal development programmes, focus may be given to the Paniya community because they are far behind than other tribal communities by all means.

References

Burman, B.K. (1973), "Modernization of Tribal People on Indian Boarders", in K.S. Mathur (ed.), 'Studies in Social Change', Lucknow: Ethnographic and Folk Culture Society, pp. 25-36.

Chandrasekhar, C.P. (2015), "Revisiting Rural Indebtedness", *Frontline*.

Delvin, J.F. (2005), "A Detailed Study of Financial Exclusion in UK", *Journal of Consumer Policy*, 28(1), pp. 75-108.

Kumar, B. (2013), "Financial Exclusion among the Tribes: A Study of Wayanad District in Kerala", Kottayam: Thesis Submitted to M.G. University (unpublished).

Mohan, Rakesh (2006), "Economic Growth, Financial Deepening and Financial Inclusion", Address to Annual Banker Conference at Hyderabad, November 3.

Nair, Ramy (2012), "India Lags behind Emerging Nations in

Financial Inclusion", available at: http://originwww.livemint.com/Industry/ZLqb6dEHp9nav1Osub WJQL/India-lagsbehindemerging-nations-in-financial-inclusion.html.

RBI (2005), "Taking Banking Services to the Common Man for Financial Inclusion", Commemorative Lecture by Shri V. Leeladhar, Deputy Governor Reserve Bank of India at the Fedbank Hormis Memorial Foundation, Ernakulam, December 2.

World Bank (2007), "Finance for All: Policy and Pitfalls in Expanding Access," Policy Research Report, available at: http://www.goWorld Bank.org/4YSZ5KS6CO.

World Bank (2009), "Global Innovation Policy Course: Introduction to Innovation Policy", World Bank, Washington D.C.

Worthington, Andrew C. (2006), "Predicting Financial Literacy in Australia", Faculty of Commerce, School of Accounting and Finance, University of Banking Group Limited (ANZ), Australia.

7

Empowering Poor through Financial Inclusion

S.N. Tripathy

Introduction

Micro finance is the prerequisite of a broad range of financial services such as deposits, loans, payment services, money transfers and insurance to poor and low income households and their micro enterprises. Financial service is one of the key pillars for the holistic development of poor, enabling them to access finance and empowering them in leading a life with dignity. The poor and the underprivileged need a numerous range of financial instruments to be capable to build assets, stabilize consumption and protect themselves against risks. Micro finance has emerged as an important mechanism of empowering the poor by enabling access to financial services and facilitating their involvement in the economic activities. Micro finance affects women's ability or decision-making and self-confidence which are closely linked to knowledge, women status and their gender relations at home. Micro finance programme strengthens women's economic autonomy while giving them the means to pursue non-traditional activities.

SHG-Bank Linkage Programme

In the last two and half decades, the major institutional innovation in India for expanding financial system access and its usage by the poor and marginalized sections of the population has been the SHG-Bank Linkage Programme (SBLP). This was an outcome of pilot projects during the 1980s for improving access of rural poor to formal institutional financial services. For the banks, it was a way of reducing their transaction costs by dealing with groups of people rather than individuals, reducing the credit risks through peer pressure and making people save.

Subsequently in the year 1992, the National Bank for Agriculture and Rural Development (NABARD) started a pilot project of linking SHGs with branches of banks across the country. The project provided a cost-effective SBLP model for providing financial services to the underserved poor. Being a 'savings-first, credit later' model, credit discipline became a norm for SHGs and 'social collateral' made them bankable. The model was also successful in providing solution to the twin problems faced by banks, i.e., low recovery of loans in rural areas and high transaction costs in dealing with small borrowers at frequent intervals. One of the major positive impacts of the SBLP was social and economic empowerment of the members. Thus, the self-help group (SHG) movement in India has enabled social and economic inclusion of women. The SHG-Bank Linkage movement, where SHGs are linked to banks in a gradual way—initially through savings and later through loan products—has been able to ensure financial inclusion to a certain extent.

Review of Literature

It is conceived that there has been no dearth of studies on the issue of micro finance and financial inclusion (FI) in India. Several researchers have concluded that micro credit is an effective device for empowering women in the present period (Mayoux, 1998, 1999; Kabeer, 1998; Goetz and Sengupta 1996; Mayoux, 2001). They also argue that micro credit has the potential to increase women empowerment through decision on mobility. However, we can outline a few studies on FI so as to find out the gap existing in research, thereby justifying the present study.

Friedman (1992) defined empowerment in terms of "inclusion" and "exclusion" and central importance of "power" in a political sense, not merely limited to a particular development activity. The involvement of women groups in development projects at the grassroots levels through direct involvement in the decision-making and implementation process empowers them. It also contributes to the chance of them contributing their own efforts to the mainstream of the development of their communities.

According to Murdoch (1999), micro finance is a useful tool for the empowerment of women and the poor. It is an essential weapon for alleviation of poverty and certainly an ideal approach for developing economies to solve women's difficulties in obtaining finance.

Schreiner and Colombet (2001) defined micro finance as "an attempt to improve access to small deposits and small loans for poor households neglected by banks". In other words, micro finance is to cater for the un-served working population in the rural and backward regions by making accessible, dependable financial services to the poor and low income groups. Micro finance has been a viable cost-effective mechanism for providing financial services to the poor and low income households, in meeting their financial requirements for the purpose of income generating activities.

Mawa (2008) found that micro credit has had a positive effect on national development but could not reach poorest of the poor. Extremely poor were being excluded from micro credit programmes by peer screening; group members were not willing to extend finance to the extremely poor for the fear that the loans will not be repaid on time or not repaid at all.

Reji (2009) in his study found a significant improvement in living standard and confidence level of the members especially in the context of micro finance and decision-making through the micro finance program. He found that more than 75 percent women members took part in decision-making related to credit and savings, income generating activities, acquisition of new goods, children's education, marriage of children, and selection of jobs and so on.

Karmakar et al. (2011) made an effort in assessing

financial inclusion in India and emphasized the need to expand the reach of formal financial institutions such as banks, as a channel for access to a range of financial services. The study also focused on the role of technological innovations in bringing down the costs of provision of services.

Sarma and Pais (2011) analysed the cross-section data from several dozen countries to study the factors associated with financial inclusion. They found that levels of human development and financial inclusion are positively correlated. More precisely, lower income inequality, higher literacy levels and better physical and communication infrastructure are all associated with greater financial inclusion.

Tripathy (2017) found that there has been a high level of awareness of the gender magnitudes and in this perspective; women's empowerment has gained momentum. Before inception of micro credit in these areas, women in these study villages were not used to assembling and talking collectively around issues.

But the formation of SHG groups provided the basis for such social gatherings through a collective process leading to their active involvement and participation in development related activities. These in turn, ultimately created conducive and positive synergies that were more likely to break the cycle of impoverishment among the sample villages of SHG households in the KBK region of Odisha.

Tripathy (2018) encapsulated that micro finance has emerged as an important mechanism for delivery of financial services to the poor. However, there are problems for the micro finance institutions in the form of regulatory and supervisory indifferences which leads to financial exclusion of a large segment of the poor. However, there exists a huge market for financial services with regards to loans and savings.

It is inferred from above analysis that though there is plethora of studies on FI through micro finance but there is paucity of studies pertaining to the ongoing trends of FI and the role of technology in accelerating FI.

Objectives of the Study

In the light of the above backdrop, the present study has the following objectives:

- To outline the background, objectives and methodology of the study;
- To focus on the role and rationale of financial inclusion in empowering the poor; and
- To illustrate the ongoing trends, the role of the Reserve Bank of India (RBI) and the use of technology in accelerating the tempo of financial inclusion.

Methodology

The paper outlines the basic ingredients of financial inclusion, and its essentiality for empowering the poor to attain socio-economic development. The study concentrates on the role of financial inclusion in reaching out to the poor and the unserved. The study is exclusively based on secondary sources including reports of the RBI, NABARD, books on financial inclusion and related research papers.

Empowerment of Poor

Empowerment is a multi-dimensional social process that helps people to gain control over their own lives. Empowerment occurs within the sociological psychological economic spheres and also at various other levels, such as individual, groups and community. It challenges our assumptions about status quo, asymmetrical power relationship and social dynamics. Empowering women puts the focus on education and employment which are essential elements to sustainable development.

Micro finance plays a major role in gender and development strategy because of its direct relationship with both poverty alleviation and women. As women are the poorest of the poor, greater financial security allows them to become independent and empowered in household and community affairs. This is because women spend most of their income on their family needs particularly children's education, diet, health care and clothing. Proponents of women empowerment argue that repayment record of women and their cooperative behaviour are better than their counterparts i.e. men. Access to financial services empowers women by enabling them to access material (credit, property, and money), human, and social resources (education, business).

Financial Inclusion

Financial inclusion has been defined as the process of ensuring access to financial services and timely and adequate credit where needed by vulnerable groups such as weaker sections and low income groups at an affordable cost (The Committee on Financial Inclusion, Dr. C. Rangarajan).

In the context of financial inclusion, it broadens the resource base of the financial system by developing a culture of savings among a large segment of rural population and plays its own role in the process of economic development. Further, by bringing low income groups within the perimeter of formal banking sector; financial inclusion protects their financial wealth and other resources in exigent circumstances. Financial inclusion also mitigates the exploitation of vulnerable sections by the usurious money lenders by facilitating easy access to formal credit. Financial inclusion acts as a facilitator in the holistic development of poor by empowering them to ameliorate their living conditions.

Significance of Financial Inclusion

The concept of financial inclusion has a special significance for a growing economy like India, as bringing a large segment of the productive sectors of the economy under formal financial network could unleash creative capacities besides augmenting domestic demand on a sustainable basis driven by income and consumption growth from such sectors. Financial inclusion efforts do have multiplier effect on the economy as a whole through higher savings pooled from the vast segment of the bottom of the pyramid (BoP) population by providing access to formal savings arrangement resulting in expansion in credit and investment by banks. Government also immensely benefits by way of efficient and leakage-proof transfer of vast amounts of welfare benefits to the targeted, disadvantaged groups of the population.

The concept of financial inclusion has a distinctive implication for a growing economy like India due to the fact that effective implementation of financial inclusion covers a large segment of the poor/low income groups for financial services. It encompasses productive sectors of the economy; under formal financial network; unleashes their creative capacities besides enhancing domestic demand on a viable basis driven by income and consumption growth. Better financial inclusion further leads to improvement of the financial conditions of the poor and lower income groups by enhancing their living standards, enabling them to create financial assets, generate income and build resilience to adapt to macroeconomic and livelihood shocks.

Financial inclusion broadens the resource base of the financial system by developing a culture of savings among a large segment of rural population and plays its own role in the process of economic development. Further, by bringing low income groups within the perimeter of formal banking sector; financial inclusion protects their financial wealth and other resources in crucial circumstances. Financial inclusion also mitigates the exploitation of vulnerable sections by the usurious money lenders by facilitating easy access to formal credit.

Financial inclusion supports in attaining development by enabling financial services to the unreached people with the help of banks and financial institutions. Access to financial services plays a critical role in development by facilitating economic growth and reducing income inequality. Financial inclusion enables poor people to save and to borrow, allowing them to build their assets, to invest in education and entrepreneurial ventures, and thus, improve their standard of living. It promotes thrift and develops culture of saving and also enables efficient payment mechanism strengthening the resource base of the financial institutions which benefits the economy as resources become available for efficient payment mechanism and allocation. Apart from these minimum basic products, banks can also offer other products like insurance, mutual funds, etc. to the account holders.

RBI Initiatives towards Financial Inclusion

The RBI has been the guiding spirit in implementing financial inclusion and as such, pursuing a multi-pronged strategy for enhancing the outreach of financial services including the delivery channels across all sections. The entire spectrum of the financial system which comprises of commercial banks, regional rural banks (RRBs), urban co-operative banks (UCBs), primary agricultural credit societies (PACS) and post offices is, therefore, geared for this purpose. Besides, self-help groups (SHGs) and micro finance institutions (MFIs) also meet the financial service requirements of the poorer segments. Furthermore, banks have been stimulated to use a combination of strategies which include provision of new products.

Under the advice of the Reserve Bank, SCBs have embarked upon a three-year financial inclusion plan (FIP) consistent with their business strategies and comparative advantages as an integral part of their corporate plans. FIP comprises of self-set targets to enlarge their outreach in terms of outlets and customer base as well as to offer a range of products suited for the purpose. They embrace specific goals for coverage of unbanked villages, opening of accounts and other specific products aimed at financially excluded segments. Banking penetration has improved significantly and the gap across various geographical regions has declined on account of the efforts made by RBI towards expanding access to the formal financial system. It is heartening to note that under-banked geographical regions such as the North-East as well as the eastern and central regions recorded noteworthy improvement in population per bank branch. Complementing the focused efforts of the government, RBI is propagating financial literacy, which lends sustainability to the inclusion process.

The RBI had constituted the committee in July 2015 headed by RBI Executive Director Deepak Mohanty, with a view to examining the existing policy regarding FI and formed a five year (medium-term) action plan. It was assigned to suggest strategies on several components with regard to payments, deposits, credit, social security transfers, pension and insurance which are enumerated below:

1. Augment the government social cash transfer system in order to increase the personal disposable incomes of the poor. It would put the economy on a medium-term sustainable inclusion path.
2. Banks should make special efforts to step up account opening for females belonging to lower income groups under Sukanya Shiksha Scheme for social cash transfers.
3. Aadhaar should be linked to each individual credit account as a unique biometric identifier which can be shared with TransUnion CIBIL to enhance the stability of the credit system and improve access.
4. Bank's traditional business model should be changed with greater reliance on mobile technology to improve 'last mile' service delivery.
5. It should be implemented in order to increase formal credit supply to all agrarian segments through Aadhaar-linked mechanism for credit eligibility certificates (CECs).
6. Corporates should be encouraged to nurture SHGs as a part of corporate social responsibility (CSR) initiative.
7. Government should replace current agricultural input subsidies on fertilizers, irrigation and power by a direct income transfer scheme as a part of second generation reforms.
8. Government should introduce universal crop insurance scheme covering all crops starting with small and marginal farmers with monetary ceiling of ₹ 2 lakh.

9. It should also be encouraged to provide credit guarantees in niche areas for micro, small and medium enterprises (MSMEs). It would also explore possibilities for counter guarantee and re-insurance. It should be introduced for all MSME borrowers and information from it should be shared with the credit bureaus.

Emerging Technologies and Financial Inclusion

There is no denying and there is also abundant empirical evidence from within the micro finance sector and outside that technology helps in the long-run in bringing down the operational costs. However, in the micro finance space, it is imperative to conceive that technology per se is not a social intervention; the social character comes to it though the client centric organizations that use technology for elevating the poor.

Hence, the financial inclusion strategy largely focuses on the use of information and communication technology (ICT) to expand access to banking facilities through business correspondent (BCs), who carry a hand-held device which is networked to the bank's systems.

Currently, in the wake of emerging technologies, and rising MF client's expectations, the FI process reshaped the way the business is to be performed and propelled the FI processes higher up the value chain, augmenting the capabilities.

The advent of technological innovation with the introduction of information technology and cell phone coupled with IT-enabled services has emerged as a viable solution for greater financial inclusion. As a result, the combination of these technologies minimises the need and cost of both setting up of physical branches and banking personnel at various locations to cater to the needs of the customers.

The banking sector has made rapid strides largely because of the swift advancement in technology which has resulted in significant improvements in consumer experience and has also helped banks in widening their outreach. Automated teller machines, internet and mobile banking, payment wallets, and other advancements have brought in significant improvements in consumer experience. The recent developments in banking technology have transformed banking from the traditional brick-and-mortar infrastructure like staffed branches, to a system accompanied by other channels like automated teller machines (ATMs), credit/debit cards, online money transactions, internet banking, etc.

Most banks have started issuing smart cards to people in rural areas to initiate financial inclusion. These cards eliminate the need to visit bank branches to deposit and withdraw money, as banks appoint business correspondents to regularly visit the assigned villages.

Banks can consider reinforcing their capabilities by using the huge amount of transactional data to consolidate customer data, digitise business processes quickly and continuously evaluate new technologies through dedicated innovation labs or partnership models. Several banks have introduced apps that squeeze the key functionalities of a bank into a smart phone.

Table 7.1 shows the growing trends and growth in financial inclusion for the period 2013 to 2016 through installation of ATMs, expansion of bank branches, opening of deposit and loan accounts with commercial banks etc.

The expansion of financial services to all sections of the society (financial inclusion) is more significant, in order to leverage development and growth benefits. The crucial problem in attaining substantial financial inclusion is the cost of serving the small value, unprofitable customer segments or providing credit facilities to those with irregular income history.

Constraints in the Way of Financial Inclusion

Access to financial products is constrained by several factors which consist of: (i) lack of awareness about the financial products, (ii) unaffordable products, (iii) high transaction costs, and products which are not convenient, and (iv) inflexible products, not customized and of low quality etc.

Table 7.1: Indian Approach to Financial Inclusion: Trends and Growth

Indicators	2013	2014	2015	2016
Automated Teller Machines (ATMs) per 100,000 adults	12.87	17.80	19.70	21.24
Branches of commercial banks per 100,000 adults	11.85	12.87	13.54	14.06
Deposit accounts with commercial banks per 1,000 adults	1,160.72	1,337.41	1,541.79	1,731.27
Loan accounts with commercial banks per 1,000 adults	142.48	151.27	154.45	170.77
Mobile money transactions: number per 1,000 adults	36.32	117.21	273.05	635.22

Source: *Report of the Working Group on FinTech and Digital Banking*, Reserve Bank of India, 2018.

1. Financial illiteracy is also one of the formidable challenges in the sphere of financial inclusion. Lack of basic education prevents people in accessing host of financial services. Moreover, access to formal financial services requires various documents of proof regarding persons' identity, income, birth certificates, etc. But poor people generally lack these documents and thus are devoid of these financial services and the associated benefits.
2. There are problems like non-availability of appropriate banking technology, lack of proper physical infrastructure, digital connectivity, etc. in some parts of the country. If financial inclusion is to take place, it can only be through information and communication technology (ICT) based models. But there are constraints in the way of financial inclusion. It has been extensively recognized that it is not feasible to have physical banking facility in every habitation.
3. Poor people residing even in urban areas/slums do not completely exploit the financial services made available to them by banks, because they find them costly and unaffordable which prevent the poor from accessing them.
4. Many financial institutions and banks are unable to justify on commercial grounds the establishment of broad-based

infrastructure to serve poor households. As a result of this, they sometimes pull back to their physical presence in rural areas and place some limits like high minimum account balance which discourages poor people. Consequently, they also pass the additional cost on to the customers, who had to travel to distant branches and encounter long que time. As a result, many poor people abandon financial inclusion which in their opinion serves the middle and the upper classes only.

Conclusion

A perusal of the above analysis brings to light that while the benefits of growth due to reforms, have concentrated in the hands of those who are already served by the formal financial system, a large section of the rural poor nevertheless does not have access to the formal banking channels.

In the above backdrop, it must be taken into consideration that financial inclusion is a powerful enabler of inclusive economic growth. Thus, in recent years financial inclusion, has undergone a paradigm shift; keeping pace with successive waves of technological changes, and evolving in tune with the needs of the nation. It has been established that access to finance and financial services empowers people in many ways.

Policy Implications

Expansion of financial inclusion requires focused efforts to be carried out in partnership with all stakeholders including private sector banks and through effective national strategic policies involving the rural poor and micro enterprises that are under-serviced/unreached by the banks.

In the absence of transactional banking services, financing to the poor will be insecure and costly because the underprivileged people cannot participate wholly in the economy either as consumers or as micro enterprisers. In this context, financial inclusion needs to be supplemented by a policy package of comprehensive social protection programs;

minimizing the risks and vulnerability arising from economic crises and natural calamities.

A holistic pro-poor approach is to be adhered to which will facilitate in breaking the vicious inter-generational cycles of poverty and hunger. It will reduce widening disparities between the rich and the poor. The policy packages should have inbuilt mechanism of covering wide range of issues like developing capacities at the human and institutional levels so as to implement and enforce policies effectively towards a better and effective financial inclusion.

Windows of opportunities need to be created and complemented in order to facilitate effective financial inclusion. For the success of expeditious and time bound implementation of financial inclusion, capacity development efforts need to be focussed on such aspects like: (a) offsetting the risk of new products for the commercial sector, (b) creating greater access to unreached consumers, (c) introducing new technology, (d) enhancing consumers' financial and technical education, (e) bringing in private sector entrepreneurial skills to improve financial infrastructure, and (f) setting service and credit standards. It is imperative to create an enabling environment for attracting investments, ensuring competition, augmenting equity, inclusiveness and social protection, use of new technologies and facilitating new markets.

Effective engagements of the BoP/under-banked population in the economy through the formal financial system could lead to improvement of their financial conditions and living standards, enabling them to create financial assets, generate income and build resilience to meet macroeconomic shocks.

In this context, as the access to micro credit/finance and associated advantages leads to FI; it has been aptly suggested that "micro-credit has to be necessarily accompanied by other social security schemes such as Mahatma Gandhi Rural Employment Guarantee Act, supply of subsidised food grains under the National Food Security Mission, micro-pension schemes, and subsidised healthcare. For micro credit itself to succeed as an effective tool of financial empowerment and to facilitate sustainable rural micro enterprises, the same has to be built around specific livelihoods which have a strong linkage support, are promoted by efficient NGOs/ intermediaries with a strong institutional machinery and support system, and the process envisages building of strong institutional support system". (Mani and Tandon, 2015)

References

Friedman, J. (1992), "Empowerment: The Politics of Alternative Development", Oxford Blackwell.

Goetz, A.M. and Sengupta, R. (1996), "Who takes Credit? Gender, Power, and Control over Loan Use in Rural Credit Programmes in Bangladesh", *World Development*, 24, (1), pp. 45- 63.

Gyanendra Mani and Tandon, Suparna (2015), "Microfinance in Distressed Areas of J&K, Rajasthan and Andhra Pradesh: Some Issues", *The Microfinance Review*, July-December.

Kabeer, N. (1998), "Can't Buy Me Love? Re-evaluating Gender, Credit and Empowerment in Rural Bangladesh", IDS Discussion Paper No. 363, Institute of Development Studies, Sussex.

Karmakar, K.G., Banerjee, G.D. and Mohapatra, N. (2011), "Towards Financial Inclusion in India", New Delhi: Sage Publications.

Mawa, B. (2008), "Impact of Micro Finance: Towards Achieving Poverty Alleviation", *Pakistan Journal of Social Sciences*, 5(9), pp. 876-882.

Mayoux, L. (1998), "Participatory Learning for Women Empowerment in Microfinance Programmes: Negotiating Complexity, Conflict and Change", *IDS Bulletin*, 29(4), pp. 39-50.

Mayoux, L. (1999), "Questioning Virtuous Spirals: Microfinance and Women Empowerment in Africa", *Journal of International Development*, 11, pp. 957-984.

Murdoch, J. (1999), "The Microfinance Promise", *Journal of Economic Literature*, 37, (4), pp. 1569-1614.

Rangarajan, C. (2008), "Report of the Committee on Financial Inclusion", Ministry of Finance, Government of India.

Reji, E.M. (2009), "Socio-economic Impact of Microfinance: A

Study of Neighbourhood Groups (NHGs) in Nilambur Block of Malappuram District, Kerala", *Indian Journal of Agricultural Economics*, 64(2).

Reserve Bank of India (2017), "Report on Trend and Progress of Banking in India, 2016-17", Mumbai.

Reserve Bank of India (2018), "Report of the Working Group on FinTech and Digital Banking", Mumbai.

Sarma, M. and Pais, J. (2011), "Financial Inclusion and Development", *Journal of International Development*, 23(5), pp. 613-628.

Schreiner, M. and Colombet, H. (2001), "From Urban to Rural: Lessons for Microfinance from Argentina", *Development Policy Review*, Vol. 19, No. 3, pp. 339-354.

Tripathy, S.N. (2017), "Microfinance in Empowering Tribal Women: Evidence from the Villages of KBK Districts (Odisha)", *Journal of Land and Rural Studies*, Vol. 5, Issue 2, Centre for Rural Studies, LBSNAA, Sage Publications.

Tripathy, S.N. (2018), "Micro finance and Women Empowerment", LAMBERT Academic Publishing (Omni Scriptum Publishing Group), Germany, pp. 46-74.

8

Dimensions of Financial Inclusion in India

M.H. Wani and Arshad Bhat

Introduction

Financial inclusion is defined as extension of banking and financial services to each and every individual in the society without any discrimination. It primarily aims to include everybody in the society by giving them basic financial services without looking at a person's income or savings. Financial inclusion chiefly focuses on providing reliable financial solutions to the economically underprivileged sections of the society without having any unfair treatment. Financial inclusion wants everybody in the society to be involved and participate in financial management in a judicious manner. There are many poor households in India that do not have any access to financial services in the country. They are not aware of banks and their functions. Even if they are aware of banks, many of the poor people do not have the access to get services from banks. Banks have requirements such as minimum income, minimum credit score, age criteria, and minimum years of work experience.

Financial inclusion aims to eliminate these barriers and provide economically priced financial services to the less fortunate sections of the society so that they can be financially independent without depending on charity or other means of getting funds that are actually not sustainable. Financial inclusion also intends to spread awareness about financial services and financial management among people of the society.

Importance of Financial Inclusion

Despite India boasting of economic growth rates higher than most developed countries in recent years, a majority of the country's population still remains unbanked. Financial inclusion is a relatively new socio-economic concept in India that aims to change this dynamic by providing financial services at affordable costs to the underprivileged, who might not otherwise be aware of or able to afford these services. Global trends have shown that in order to achieve inclusive development and growth, the expansion of financial services to all sections of the society is of utmost importance.

As a whole, financial inclusion in the rural as well as financially backward pockets of cities is a win-win opportunity for everybody involved—the banks/NBFCs, intermediaries, and the left-out urban population. Banks will handle core infrastructure and services while intermediaries known as business correspondents (BCs) will be the executors and act as the face of these banking and financial institutions in dealing with the end-users. The business correspondents (BCs) shall be carrying handheld terminals like tablets (GSM-enabled) coupled with portable biometric scanner, smart card swipe machines as well as thermal bluetooth printers for carrying out their online banking activities on the field. Authentication and customer information is provided by the UIDAI through NPCI or NSDL once the institution becomes an authorized UIDAI user. As income levels and consequently, savings in rural areas increase, it is essential to help earners manage their funds and facilitate incoming and outgoing payments. Allowing people to create simple, no-frills current and savings accounts, relaxing KYC norms and directly crediting social benefits to account owners will bolster an inclusive approach to finance and banking in rural areas.

Benefits of Financial Inclusion

Financial inclusion of the unbanked masses is a critical step that requires political will, bureaucratic support and constant pressure by the RBI. It is expected to unleash the hugely untapped potential of the bottom-of-pyramid section of the Indian economy.

- The rural masses will get access to banking services like cash deposits, cash payments, balance enquiry and statement of account which can be completed using fingerprint authentication. The confidence of fulfilment is provided by issuing an online receipt to the customer.
- Reduction in cash economy as more money is brought into the banking system.
- It inculcates the habit to save, thus increasing capital formation in the country and giving it an economic boost.
- Direct cash transfers to beneficiary bank accounts, instead of physical cash payments against subsidies will become possible. This also ensures that the funds actually reach the intended recipients instead of being siphoned off along the way.
- Availability of adequate and transparent credit from formal banking channels will foster the entrepreneurial spirit of the masses to increase output and prosperity in the countryside.

Hence, it is believed that financial inclusion can initiate the next revolution of growth and prosperity. In the 21st century, India has been pulling all the right levers to advance financial inclusion and economic citizenship by channelling its own transactions to lubricate the system. India's journey towards economic ascension relies on how the 65 percent unbanked population of India (conservative 2012 estimate by the World Bank) is enabled with financial infrastructure.

Schemes of Financial Inclusion in India

The Government of India has introduced several schemes for the purpose of financial inclusion. These schemes intend to provide social security to the less fortunate sections of the society. After a lot of planning and research by several financial experts and policymakers, the government launched schemes keeping financial inclusion in mind. These schemes have been launched over different years. The schemes of financial inclusion prevalent in the country are as under:

1. Pradhan Mantri Jan Dhan Yojana (PMJDY).
2. Atal Pension Yojana (APY).
3. Pradhan Mantri Vaya Vandana Yojana.
4. Stand Up India Scheme.
5. Pradhan Mantri Mudra Yojana.
6. Pradhan Mantri Suraksha Bima Yojana (PMSBY).
7. Sukanya Samriddhi Yojana.
8. Jeevan Suraksha Bandhan Yojana.
9. Credit Enhancement Guarantee Scheme (CEGS) for Scheduled Castes (SCs).
10. Venture Capital Fund for Scheduled Castes under the Social Sector Initiatives.
11. Varishtha Pension Bima Yojana (VPBY).

Special Financial Products for Financial Inclusion

Keeping in mind that low income people living in rural and urban areas have very limited access to financial products and services, scheduled commercial banks (SCBs) have been asked by the Reserve Bank of India to design and offer exclusive financial products to the economically weaker sections of the society. Many of them are only aware of basic financial services such as savings schemes, savings accounts, personal loans, crop loans, micro finance, etc. They do not know anything about credit cards or debit cards. However, due to their lack of access to instant credit facilities, banks were instructed to issue cost-efficient credit cards to the low income groups of the society. Some of the special financial products provided to them include the following.

General Credit Cards (GCCs): Banks were asked by the RBI to launch and offer General Credit Card facilities with an amount of up to ₹ 25,000 at their branches located in semi-urban and rural areas.

Kisan Credit Cards (KCCs): The Reserve Bank of India also instructed banks to provide Kisan Credit Cards exclusively to small farmers who earn very low incomes and who have very limited funds due to which they cannot invest in proper farming tools, fertilisers, pesticides, crop seeds, tractors, land for farming, storage warehouses, etc. They are forced to rely on wealthy landlords or money lenders for getting funds to sow crops. These Kisan Credit Cards are intended to help farmers make instant purchases whenever required. Many a time, farmers give up on purchasing things required for their occupation due to lack of funds.

ICT-Based Accounts via BCs: The Reserve Bank of Idnia also devised a plan to help banks to reach out to the unbanked individuals of the society by offering information and communications technology (ICT)-based bank accounts with the help of business correspondents (BCs). These accounts allow users to make withdrawals of cash, create deposits, and apply for loans and other forms of credit through electronic forms. This type of account makes banking inexpensive and simple.

Increase in ATMs: The Reserve Bank of India also reported that many rural parts of the nation do not have enough automated teller machines (ATMs) and this is hampering buying and selling operations of the people residing in those areas. In order to increase the availability of physical cash for these people, the number of ATMs has been increased massively.

Objectives of Financial Inclusion in India

The basic objectives of financial inclusion in India are as follows:

1. Financial inclusion proposes to help people secure financial services and products at economical prices including deposits, fund transfer services, loans, insurance, payment services, etc.
2. Aims to establish proper financial institutions to cater to the needs of the poor people. These institutions should have clear-cut regulations and should maintain high standards that are existent in the financial industry.
3. Aims to build and maintain financial sustainability so that the less fortunate people have a certainty of funds which they struggle to have.

4. Intends to have numerous institutions that offer affordable financial assistance so that there is sufficient competition so that clients have a lot of options to choose from. There are traditional banking options in the market. However, the number of institutions that offer inexpensive financial products and services is very minimal.
5. Intends to increase awareness about the benefits of financial services among the economically underprivileged sections of the society.
6. The process of financial inclusion works towards creating financial products that are suitable for the less fortunate people of the society.
7. Intends to improve financial literacy and financial awareness in the country.
8. Aims to bring in digital financial solutions for the economically underprivileged people of the nation.
9. Intends to bring in mobile banking or financial services in order to reach the poorest people living in extremely remote areas of the country.
10. Aims to provide tailor-made and custom-made financial solutions to poor people as per their individual financial conditions, household needs, preferences, and income levels.

Women Empowerment and Financial Inclusion

The vision of financial inclusion is inherently particular about including women in financial management activities. Financial inclusion strategies encompass the idea that women are more capable of handling finances efficiently compared to men. Hence, financial inclusion activities target women by helping them get started by engaging in financial management. There are many households where women are not permitted to be involved in managing finances. They are controlled by the men of the household and women are asked to take care of only the domestic chores.

Many conservative people in India believe that women are not capable of handling money. With the help of financial inclusion, the government, as well as non-governmental agencies, intend to get rid of this mentality. Financial inclusion roll out is encouraging women to take up more employment opportunities and be financially independent. It also explains that women will not have to rely only on men for money.

Financial inclusion intends to empower women belonging to low income groups by increasing financial awareness among them. Women are also taught in simple ways to save their money for future purposes. They are provided with exposure to multiple affordable savings instruments. They are also taught about the various forms of credit available in the market. These forms of credit will help them start up a new small business ventures or take up a training courses to apply for a new occupation. This will resultantly help in augmenting their monthly incomes.

Financial inclusion is also making many women get mobile phones for their own usage. In several parts of the nation, only men had their own mobile phones and women had to depend on these men. Over the past few years, women have started to own mobile phones and have started to use them for work purposes, business purposes, and financial requirements. Many of them have started to utilise digital modes of payment and other financial operations with the help of mobile phones. This has simplified and quickened their transactions.

The idea of financial inclusion is encouraging banks and other financial institutions to assist the unbanked sections of the society. Many of these institutions are also focussing on making women financially independent by providing special rates and exclusive discounts or other benefits. Many banks charge subsidised or discounted interest rates from women for their loan products. For savings accounts offered by certain banks and non-banking financial corporations, women depositors gain more on interest on their deposits when compared to men.

Digital Payment Systems and Financial Inclusion

People can also make payments for products and services in their residential regions with the help of electronic payment wallet systems. The Government of India has launched several electronic wallet systems through smart phone apps such as Bharat Interface for Money (BHIM), Aadhaar Pay, and lots more. Electronic wallets or e-wallets refer to wallets that can be used with the help of electronic means such as mobile phones. These wallets replace physical wallets. A user can make cashless payments through online as well as offline mode. He or she will need to download the e-wallet app on their mobile phone and utilise it to make transactions. These e-wallets can be utilised for mobile recharges, utility bill payments, grocery stores, e-commerce portals, etc.

Many digital financial tools offer attractive offers and discounts when people make use of these tools. These are very helpful and new to the economically underprivileged sections of the society. They can enjoy offers, receive cash back options, and earn rewards. These incentives will help a user to save a lot of money.

Impact of Demonetisation on Financial Inclusion

With the objective of making India completely cashless in a few years, the government has introduced inexpensive e-wallet options so that the less fortunate people of the nation are not excluded from going cashless. These e-wallets can be accessed in regional languages also apart from English. The users can select the language that he or she knows and make use of the app conveniently. Some of these e-wallets not only allow a user to make payments, but also enable them to make fund transfers from one bank account to another.

With the implementation of the demonetisation process in India in the year 2016, the need for digital financial services has risen. The ban on usage of ₹ 500 and ₹ 1,000 notes led to an increasing demand for alternate modes of payment for goods and services. Hence, the number of digital wallets increased extensively in the country. The goal of the Indian government is to make the nation cashless and hence, the high number of digital wallets is excellently helping the government in attaining its goal. Moreover, there was a rise in the transaction limit for electronic wallets to ₹ 20,000.

Many people belonging to low income groups also started to utilise electronic wallet options as they did not have any other choice. It is true that a lot of them struggled initially due to the demonetisation process. Several middle-class and low-class people were left stranded when the demonetisation process came into effect suddenly. However, the introduction of multiple digital banking and financial services served as a great boon to all economic classes of the society. Several low income people, unemployed people (including people who were illiterates) living in both rural and urban areas started to learn about how to open a bank account, how to apply for credit, how to use technology for banking services, how to avail financial services without standing in long lines, and how to carry out transactions without carrying cash in hand.

Operations of Financial Inclusion in India

Under financial inclusion, the access to financial sources can be broadly divided into credit, wealth creation, and contingency planning.

- Under the credit aspect, a low income individual needs proper access to emergency loans, consumer loans, housing loans, and business livelihood loans at affordable rates.
- Under the wealth creation aspect, a poor individual should be able to make excellent savings and have access to reliable investment options that generate good returns. Every low income household should also have basic financial literacy and understand the concept of risk in finance clearly.
- Under the contingency planning segment of the financial inclusion system, a poor person should have access to funds that can be utilised exclusively in the future. It is not enough if these people have only means to improve their income and enhance their lifestyle. They should also have

the right resources to be prepared for the future, especially when they get old. Many of the poor people may not be aware of the retirement plans. They should be provided with affordable retirement plans that will give them good returns in the later stages of their lives. They should also be given insurable contingencies to keep themselves safe and secure. They should also be given buffer savings in order to be prepared and ready for unforeseen or emergency expenses.

Micro Finance and Financial Inclusion

Micro finance is a very effective way of offering funds to the economically underprivileged sections of the society. Micro finance refers to giving micro loans or micro credit to the less fortunate entrepreneurs and small-scale business enterprises. This mode of financing has helped India extensively in achieving financial inclusion in a cost-effective manner. It has impacted the lives of the poorest people in the nation. It includes the provision of loans, savings instruments, and other financial instruments for the purpose of making more money and saving it proficiently for multiple purposes.

There are several impoverished people in the nation who do not have access to financial sources and who have no idea how to get out of their hopeless financial condition. With basic micro finance, they will be given opportunities to start some form of business or get a better job and improve their lifestyles. They do not have access to traditional banking options and hence, micro finance is a great boon to them as it gives them a chance to borrow money, utilise it for lucrative purposes, and repay it conveniently over a fixed period of time. They will also learn to manage their hard earned money meticulously.

Private Companies and Financial Inclusion

Private companies have also initiated programmes in order to contribute towards achieving financial inclusion in the nation. These private companies planned and implemented projects in order to make the low income group of people getting engaged in developmental projects.

Some of these programmes include Haryali Kisan Bazaar by DCM, E-Choupal or E-Sagar by ITC, Project Shakti by Hindustan Unilever, and many more. Over the past few years, financial inclusion has become a very prominent public policy aspect in order to develop the economy in a sustainable manner. It plays a significant role in keeping institutions that provide finance in a very steady and firm condition. Banks can enjoy excellent stability when financial inclusion is attained. It also helps in minimising the distance between financial institutions and customers, and this, in turn, assists in maintaining a healthy relationship. With financial inclusion, every economic agent in the nation will have the ability to make use of formal financial services and move towards the overall development of the economy.

References

Bakshi, P. (2012), "Financial Inclusion: BC/BF Model: What's New?", *The Journal of Indian Institute of Banking and Finance*, 83(2), pp. 5-10, available at: http://www.iibf.org.in/documents/IIB-Bank-Quest-april-june-12.pdf.

Bhaskar, P.V. (2014), "Financial Inclusion in India: An Assessment", RBI Monthly Bulletin, January, pp. 30-32, available at: http://www.rbi.org.in/scripts/BS_SpeechesView.aspx?Id=862.

Dangi, N. and Kurukshetra, P.K (2013), "Current Situation of Financial Inclusion in India and Its Future Visions", *International Journal of Management and Social Sciences Research*, 2(8), pp. 155-157.

Gandhi, M.M. (2013), "Financial Inclusion in India: Issues and Challenges", *International Multidisciplinary Journal of Applied Research*, 1(3), pp. 12-20.

Garg, Sonu and Agarwal, Parul (2014), "Financial Inclusion in India: A Review of Initiatives and Achievements", *IOSR Journal of Business and Management*, Vol. 16(6).

Joshi, Deepali Pant (2013), "Financial Inclusion", RBI Monthly Bulletin, November, pp. 133-135.

Little, A. (2012), "Data Book on Financial Inclusion", The World Bank, pp. 2-74.

Mehta, L., Jindal, S. and Singh, K. (2015), "Financial Inclusion in India: Shifting the Base towards Crowning Glory", *Arabian Journal of Business and Management Review*, Vol. 5(6).

Rangarajan, C. (2008), "Report of the Committee on Financial Inclusion", pp. 1- 31.

"Report on Trend and Progress of Banking in India, 2012-13",, Reserve Bank of India, pp. 83-87.

Singh, Nirvikar (2017), "Financial Inclusion: Concepts, Issues and Policies for India", International Growth Centre, synthesis paper.

Thapar, A. (2013), "A Study on the Effectiveness of the Financial Inclusion Program in India", *VSRD International Journal of Business and Management Research*, 3(6), pp. 211-216.

Index

Index